Australia in New Guinea, 1914

Hoisting of Flag at Rabaul, 13th September, 1914.

Australia in New Guinea, 1914

The Campaign on Land & Sea in the Pacific
During the First World War

ILLUSTRATED

Australia in Action: New Guinea, 1914
L. C. Reeves

Extract from Australasia Triumphant
A. St. John Adcock

LEONAUR

Australia in New Guinea, 1914
The Campaign on Land & Sea in the Pacific During the First World War
Australia in Action: New Guinea, 1914
by L. C. Reeves
Extract from *Australasia Triumphant*
by A. St. John Adcock

ILLUSTRATED

FIRST EDITION

Leonaur is an imprint of Oakpast Ltd

Copyright in this form © 2020 Oakpast Ltd

ISBN: 978-1-78282-908-9 (hardcover)
ISBN: 978-1-78282-909-6 (softcover)

http://www.leonaur.com

Publisher's Notes

Contents

Contents

Introduction

By Col. J. Paton, V.D., who was in command of the troops when they arrived back from New Guinea.

The success of any military expedition must be judged not from the number of casualties inflicted on the enemy or upon one's own troops, but rather upon the general results; the losses entailed in warfare are but the means towards the end in view.

Looking at the results of the Naval and Military Expeditionary Force which was despatched from Australia for the purpose of occupying the German territory in the Pacific, it will be readily conceded that the force accomplished all that was expected of them.

The short and concise narrative of events set down in this volume, and which I have just perused on the steamer today, seems to be a fairly accurate statement of incidents as they occurred from the standpoint of an individual member of the Expeditionary Force.

It will be remembered that the force hastily prepared and embarked under Col. Holmes, D.S.O., V.D., left Sydney under sealed orders, and the success of the Expedition is, of course, largely attributable to the manner in which he directed the very delicate operations and overcame the many difficulties which were necessarily encountered.

The islands now under our occupation embrace a very large area, with an immense native population and vast potentialities.

This represents the first purely Australian effort in an enterprise resulting in the military occupation of territory which must be, in the course of time, of immense value, both from a strategical and commercial standpoint.

It will be observed also that the capture of the first German war vessel (K.G.S. *Komet*) in the present war lies to the credit of this first Australian Expeditionary Force.

The perusal of this short narrative should be of particular interest to all those Australians who take such a keen interest in the doings of their sailors and soldiers.

Col. J. Paton, V.D.

S.S. *Navua*,
At Sea,
17th February, 1915.

CHAPTER 1

In Camp

When it was known in Sydney that Great Britain had declared war on Germany, the military authorities were besieged by applicants willing to go to the aid of the Motherland in her hour of danger, and when the Federal Government offered to send a force of 20,000 men for service wherever the Imperial authorities required them, the Barracks at Paddington presented a busy scene with "Sons of the Empire" eagerly enquiring for application forms and firing off all sorts of questions at the large number of officers detailed for this purpose.

By Tuesday the 11th August the enrolment and medical examination of the men offering themselves for their country's service were at their height. By 10.30 a.m. on that morning there were several hundreds inside the barrack grounds, while it was well-nigh impossible to force a passage through the waiting crowd outside the gates, where extra police, both civilian and military, had been stationed. When inside the gates, the examinees were lined up alphabetically to wait their turn to enter the big drill hall for examination by the several doctors.

Only men of the finest physique were required for active service, and nothing was to be left to chance. Each man had first been personally before Lt.-Col, Antill, who turned down all whom he considered undesirable for the duties required of them. Once inside the drill hall, the examination went on apace—eyesight, hearing, weight, height, etc., were all examined by special doctors, and if a man were even ½ or ¼ inch short of the stipulated measurements one could see the look of disappointment as the rejected one dressed and passed out.

Those who successfully passed the doctors were marched off to the Agricultural Ground in parties of eighty or a hundred. One officer took his men out of the right track, and many were the complimentary remarks passed by them as to how this particular officer might fare in an enemy's country when he could lose his bearings so easily. However, the chaff was taken good-naturedly and the men cheerfully marched back along the streets, the residents in those streets viewing Sydney's first batch of volunteers, and, no doubt, the men felt proud—although in civilian attire—as they marched along chatting light-heartedly.

The call for volunteers had been responded to by all classes, and it was a notable fact, and one generally commented upon, that, taken as a whole, the men had the appearance of holding good positions and not enlisting for the 6/- per day they were to be paid. The uniform of the "Tram Troub" was well displayed in the ranks, and as the parties marched along one heard such remarks as "Fares Please," "Hurry on Please." There were clerks, navvies, university students, miners, artificers of all trades, men who had served on the Indian frontier; ex-navy men; men who had fought on the South African *veldt* were side by side, all ready to do the Empire's bidding; ready, aye eager to help in crushing the blatant militarism of the German Empire, which, if once allowed to gain the upper hand, would kill the freedom and justice of which every Britisher is proud.

The Agricultural Ground and buildings which were to be used as barracks were eventually reached, and the men sworn in (after having been drafted into companies of one hundred and twenty men each). Instructions as to what each man was to bring into camp next morning were issued, and the men were allowed to go home.

The ensuing days of the week were occupied in knocking the men into shape; issuing rifles and equipment; appointing N.-C.O.'s., for which positions there was a good deal of competition, as there were many active service men in the ranks. Many who had held commissions under the Compulsory Training had enlisted as privates where they could not obtain a commission.

The men soon became acquainted and chummed up with one another. Those with hair of a golden hue were promptly nick-named "Blue," or " Ginger," while others received such appellations as "Broncho," "Scotty," "Tubby," "Taffy," "Yorky," "Gertie," "Snowy," "Trooper," "Darky," etc., etc.—names indicative of some characteristic of the men thus known to their comrades.

By Friday, 14th August, uniforms, rifles and equipment had been issued to the thousand men who were now encamped on the Agricultural Ground; half of them occupying the pavilion used for the exhibition of dogs at show time, while the other half were accommodated in the poultry pavilion. These building were known as the "Kennel" and the "Fowl House" respectively.

The web equipment had been served out in several pieces, which had to be put together. This presented some difficulty to all except those who had previously handled the equipment. However, these men set to, and, after putting their own equipment in order, showed the others how to join up the gear, often to find that someone else had meantime solved the difficulty by taking possession of their completed kit, leaving in its place a heap of loose buckles, straps and pouches.

The first general leave was granted on the Friday night, and very few men remained in the barracks. There were friends, relatives and sweethearts to see, for none knew but what they would receive orders to march off next morning, and the men made the most of the limited time at their disposal. Many met friends in the city, who gave their khaki clad mates a royal time, and more than one arriving back at the barracks after the stipulated hour had to sneak into the "Kennel" or "Fowl House" while the sentry looked in another direction.

The troops were paraded together as a battalion for the first time on Saturday afternoon, when they were inspected by the commanding officers. Many of the public had come out to see their soldier friends, and the men were glad when they were dismissed, as all knew only too well the time, they had at their disposal was limited.

On Sunday morning a very touching Church Parade was

held. Later on, came an examination of feet to ascertain if the boots issued were in any way uncomfortable. Corns and blisters were attended to and hints given on the care of the feet generally. The authorities wanted this force to be well and fully equipped, and bad fitting garments were to be exchanged for those of the correct size. Another parade was held in the afternoon, when the men were marched out into Centennial Park, where there was quite a large number of people who witnessed the battalion drilling and manoeuvring. Although experienced men would, no doubt, have found faults with some of the movements, it must be said that the men showed fine form when one takes into consideration the fact that they had been in camp for only four days.

General leave was granted from 5 p.m. until midnight, and the men lost no time in ridding themselves of their kits and leaving the Show Ground. Those who made an effort to pass the sentries with hats or sidearms, without belts, or with their dress incorrect in any way were turned back and made all haste to rectify the mistakes, forgetting in their hurry to say the hard words they thought about the sentries, but none the less annoyed for having their leave reduced by even three or four minutes.

Monday, 17th August, 1914, was occupied by more drilling and rifle exercises, the men being paraded and inspected in the afternoon. It was now well known throughout the ranks that the force was to be embarked on a transport next day, and the news was quickly handed round from one to another—the papers not being allowed to make any announcement of this fact. The leave granted that night was made the most of.

CHAPTER 2

Departure from Sydney

On Tuesday morning, 18th August, the force was inspected by the State Governor, Sir Gerald Strickland, who said this was the first Australian force to leave under sealed orders; not an officer or man of the whole battalion knew for what part of the world he was bound; the troops before him were a fine body of men, the pick of New South Wales, and he could conscientiously say they were as fine a lot of men as he had ever seen. Col. Watson was decorated by the governor with the V.D. medal and, headed by the band, the infantry portion of the first Australian Naval and Military Expedition moved off from the Agricultural Ground, where they had been encamped for less than a week. Company pets had this time been brought on parade, for the men were now to embark on the troopship. There were several dogs; from one pack peeped a kitten with blue ribbon and bell, while a *galah* was one company's mascot.

The band made a vast difference in the step as the men marched along in full kit—many of which were added to on the way, as presents of one kind or another were handed to the men; some for the comfort of the "soldier boy"; some dainty morsel to appease the cravings of the inner man on the earlier part of the trip; a huge pineapple, a pair of sox, coloured handkerchiefs, box of cakes, etc.

The force passed along Oxford, College and Macquarie Streets on their way to Fort Macquarie. Along Oxford Street the girls from the ribbon stores brought out rolls of red, white and blue ribbon, which was cut up and fixed on bayonet points, in hats, on sleeves—anywhere where it would show up. Flags were in evidence all along the line, practically every other man having a flag or patriotic emblem of some kind waving from his rifle. Not a few friends and relatives marched side by side in the ranks all the way from the barracks to Fort Macquarie, where hurried goodbyes were said and the men embarked on board two of the Sydney Ferries steamers *en route* for Cockatoo Island. On the heights round Fort Macquarie, in the old Government House grounds, on every vantage point were crowds of people to wish God-speed to the troops, while thousands of Sydney's citizens had witnessed the march from the barracks to the water front, and this in spite of the fact that the papers had not been permitted to publish any intimation of the expedition's departure. News travels apace.

The two large ferry boats were soon loaded with khaki clad troops, who swarmed all over the vessels, clambering on the roofs, singing songs, patriotic or sentimental, hymns, or the latest rag time melodies, as the fancy took them. The boats moved off, and this was the signal for all the steamboats in the vicinity to commence "Cock-a-doodle-doo," which was kept up almost incessantly till Cockatoo Island was reached. Each vessel passing the laden ferries was greeted by the men with three rousing British cheers until they were so hoarse, they could cheer no more. Hats and handkerchiefs were waved to all in sight on boats or foreshores. An Australian lass emerged from one house on the heights with a pair of flags and signalled, "Goodbye boys; Good luck." Needless to say, that particular house received an extra hearty cheer.

Cockatoo Island was reached without accident, and the troops got aboard the P. & O. Branch Line Steamer *Berrima*, which had been converted into Troopship No. 1, and was now designated "H.M.A. Transport *Berrima*," a vessel of 12,000 tons. She was lying in Sutherland Dock, and when once on board it was found that down 'tween decks had been fitted up with mess tables and forms, hooks for hammocks, helmets, equipment, etc. Up on the decks, hooks had also been fixed so that those who desired could swing their hammocks in the open. The forward part of the vessel had been set apart for the accommodation of some 600 naval reservists drawn from the depots at Brisbane, Sydney, Newcastle, Melbourne and Adelaide, while the troops were quartered aft. However, they had no time allowed to inspect their new home but were set to work on the stacks of stores lying on the wharf which had to be stowed away down in the holds for their sustenance in the unknown country for which they were bound.

All worked at wharf-labouring with a will, and the stacks of stores soon disappeared. Some of the men were called away to see friends or relatives who had called to say farewell to the boy in khaki. Some even managed to pass the sentries and see the men at work. One young lady sneaked in with a camera, and after taking a photo of her brother (or someone else's brother, perhaps), and a few of his comrades, an officer came along and said she must go outside, and not satisfied with this was about to confiscate the camera. However, a few words, with a promise to keep the camera out of sight, set the matter right, and the young lady went off with the photo hidden away in the camera.

Swinging hammocks caused a little trouble to some of the men at first. Some in trying to get into the hammocks forgot the movement and found themselves diving to deck and clutching at the swinging hammocks for safety. Each bump, accompanied by mixed mutterings and prayers for the hammocks, announced a fresh casualty.

By six o'clock next morning (Wednesday, 19th August), the boat was being got out of the dock and, as soon as she was clear, headed down the harbour. This was the signal for further displays of patriotic enthusiasm as the *Berrima* steamed down the harbour past Circular Quay and anchored to the *Australia's* buoy in Farm Cove, where the ferry boats from the northern suburbs passed close by, the passengers cheering, while the masters of the ferry steamers must have got tired blowing their whistles as they passed by time after time on their way to and from Manly, Watson's Bay, Balmoral, Cremorne, Mosman, Neutral. Any boat passing by and not responding to the demand of "Blow your

1. *Drilling.*   *On H.M.A.S. Berrima.*   3. *"Good-bye, Sydney Town."*
2. *Church Parade.*

Whistle," was promptly counted out, but they invariably came up to the scratch and gave the desired "Cock-a-doodle-doo."

A boat loaded with a couple of hundred men of the militia steamed round the troopship with a band playing popular airs and departed in the direction of the heads, exchanging cheers with the men aboard the *Berrima*.

Mails for the fleet were brought aboard, and about noon "H.M.A. Transport *Berrima*" moved off in the direction of the heads amidst the sound of cheerings and whistlings. The heads were cleared at 1 p.m., a quay bound Manly steamer steaming out a little way towards the heads and giving a parting blast which was acknowledged with a ringing cheer from the troopship. As the pilot boats were passed outside the whole of the men aboard the vessel were singing:—

Goodbye Sydney town;
Sydney town goodbye;
I am leaving you today
For a country far away, etc.

There were not a few moist eyes as the *Berrima* dipped into the swell, and for some little while many of the men had a strong desire to avoid their comrades.

Heading north, Manly was soon passed, and by this time the horrible complaint of sea-sickness had attacked many of the men. Those affected with the malady lay down anywhere—on the decks, on the hatches, anywhere—it didn't matter where they lay, they remained undisturbed, and many of them thought of the old song, "Mister Captain, stop the ship I want to get out and walk."

And so, departed the first Australian Expedition.

CHAPTER 3

The Voyage Along the Coast

Still heading north, the next morning land was out of sight, and during the morning the gun crews engaged in gunnery practice with the 4.7 guns which had been mounted on the troopship for defensive purposes. About midday an Orient liner was passed heading south and in the afternoon, land was sighted in the vicinity of Byron Bay.

It may not be out of place to here give a copy of the routine which was being followed on board ship:—

6.30 a.m.	Reveille.
	Wash and Cocoa.
7 to 8 a.m.	Early Morning Parade.
7.50 a.m.	Cooks.
8.10 a.m.	Breakfast.
9.30 to 12	Forenoon Parade.
10.30 a.m.	Smoke-oh.
12.10 p.m.	Cooks.
12.30 p.m.	Dinner.
2 to 4 p.m.	Afternoon Parade.
3 p.m.	Smoke-oh.
5.10. p.m.	Cooks.
5.30 p.m.	Tea.
8.30 p.m.	Stand by Hammocks.
9 p.m.	First Post.
9.30 p.m.	Last Post.
9.55 p.m.	Pipe Down.

10 p.m.   Lights out (men quiet for rest of night)

On Friday morning, 21st August, the *Berrima* entered Moreton Bay, where the anchor was dropped just inside the heads,
close beside the small gun-boat *Gayundah*, which went outside
soon after to reconnoitre. The *Berrima* remained in Moreton Bay
all day, the daily routine as laid down being gone through as
usual. The men were hoping to get ashore at Brisbane, but their
hopes were doomed to disappointment when the *Gayundah* returned to her former position about 5 p.m., and the *Berrima*
once more got under way. In turning, she ran aground on a
sand-bank—which are fairly numerous in Moreton Bay—and
it was not till very late that she was once more outside in open
water, which fact was forcibly brought home to the men by the
swaying of their hammocks in the wind which was blowing
fresh outside the bay.

Again, they were on their way, steaming northwards to their
unknown destination—unknown but generally accepted as being some one of the German possessions in the Pacific—New
Guinea or the Solomon Islands.

Saturday afternoon was placed at the disposal of the troops,
who passed the time in various ways—washing or mending
clothes; others playing cards, while a few who were the lucky
possessors of magazines put in their time reading; others again
were writing letters ready for the first mail that would be sent
away from the troopship.

About 3.30 p.m. a stir was caused when a vessel was sighted coming up from seawards. There was much conjecture as
to what vessel it was, and eventually the *Sydney* came up and
steamed along just ahead of the *Berrima* all night. Next morning
both vessels lay to in the calm sea while the mails which the *Berrima* had brought were transferred to the cruiser.

The much talked of "Barrier Reef" was sighted on the first
Sunday out, and all that day numerous coral islands and islets
were passed close by; some rising to a great height while others
were only a few feet above the water level; some thickly covered
with timber, others devoid of all vegetation. During the morning the troopship and her convoy passed within a few miles of

Nair's Rock, on which the interstate vessel, the *Yongala*, is supposed to have struck during a gale, when all on board were lost.

In the evening the *Sydney* steamed away to Townsville, leaving the *Berrima* to pursue her course without a convoy, but not for long, for when day broke the *Berrima* was lying at anchor in a sheltered bay a couple of miles off Palm Island, and H.M.S. *Encounter* was lying close by.

CHAPTER 4

Palm Island

Although only a few days since leaving Sydney, all were anxious to once more set foot on solid ground, but none dreamed that before continuing the onward journey, that they would be sick and tired of the very sound of Palm Island In the afternoon of the first day at Palm Island the motor launch and seven of the *Berrima*'s boats were lowered and loaded with troops. All seven boats were towed ashore by the little white launch, the eight vessels resembling a huge serpent gliding along on the calm surface. Some of the men were landed at a rocky point, while others were landed on a beach a few miles further round the island. The parties were marched over the steep hills and given good practice in skirmishing, scouting, etc.

The return to the *Berrima* was made at low tide, and as the water is very shallow for a long way out, the men had to wade out to the boats. Those who took off *puttees*, boots and sox kept a wary eye on oyster shells and coral, and during the stay at Palm Island several of the troops were under the care of the A.M.C. with cut feet. The walk through the shallow water to the boats was accompanied with plenty of good-natured chaff. Such remarks as "Now then, fall in," followed by "Too (Two) deep," were heard as the men marched through the water with their officers.

Then there was further amusement when the men began clambering into the boats with their full equipment on and with boots, etc., hanging round their necks. Not a few narrowly es-

Palm Island.

1. *Skirmishing on the hills.*
2. *Wading to the boats.*
3. *Entrenching practice.*

caped a complete soaking as they clung to the boat in a vain endeavour to secure a seat in the ferry. As each boat was filled it set out for the *Berrima*, the men rowing the boats back this time.

"There's a boat just ahead of us, lads." The rowers set to with a will and the boat in front was gradually overhauled. At length it was passed with a cheer and the *Encounter* drew nigh. The man-o'-war was passed within a few yards, and the men at the oars put on their best stroke and attempted to show the navy men that the land lubbers could row as well as they.

"Now lads, a steady stroke," said the coxswain, "all together— watch the stroke oar—let the tars see how you *can* pull."

Needless to say the man-o'-war was reached in fine style and then there was a terrible tangle. One oar had a tendency to keep under the water despite all efforts to get it above, and it got tangled up with the others. The men daren't look up at the *Encounter's* decks, for something told them the men in navy blue were smiling down at them.

The upshot of this little exhibition of rowing was that a challenge was received from the *Encounter* to row a boat's crew selected from the troops aboard the *Berrima*. The troops put up a good race at the start but the navy drew away and won with ease. On the following days, after the return from Palm Island, boat races were held between crews representing each company in the force, and these races in the afternoon served to pass away the time and give the men something to talk about and, to a little extent, kept the men from becoming discontented with their weary wait.

Each day ashore was much the same, the companies going overland up the steep hills, or over the rocky shore and up the gullies, in skirmishing order; the A.M.C. were able to have good practice in improvising first aid material in the bush, erecting shelters for the wounded, etc.; the signalling corps formed stations in various parts of the island and had good practice in sending messages from one point to another; the machine gun detachment got away by themselves in a gully and did their best to break all records in getting their guns ready, and also had plenty of target practice; one gully resounded with bugle calls, where all

Training at Palm Island.

the buglers had assembled to run through the many calls.

There was good water on the island, and after the warm condensed water, which was all that could be got on board ship, it was quite a treat to drink from the spring in the rocks under the trees, and on return to the *Berrima* the usual question, "Bring any water back?" would be asked by those men who had not been ashore that day. On the beach the men were able to have a refreshing dip after their day's skirmishing and before returning to their floating home. On Friday afternoon when the boats were returning to the troopship about 5 p.m., the cruiser *Sydney* came in at a good speed and dropped anchor close by. Everyone was anxious to know what was about to be done—when were the boats going to leave Palm Island?—why were they waiting there so long, etc. Naturally, many wild rumours were circulated, all obtained from "best authority."

The first mail to be despatched from the troops since their departure from Sydney closed on Friday night, and when it was known that a mail was to be sent off, paper and pencils were in great demand. "Can we get stamps?" "No! Don't want any." "Where do we post 'em?" "Got an indelible?" "Lend us an envelope, Blue." "How are you off for paper, mate?" "Got a spare envelope?" are only a few of the remarks heard. Nearly everyone had someone to write a letter to, while a few required a special mail bag to convey the letters they had written.

On the 30th August a fourth vessel entered the harbour and dropped anchor. It was the E. & A. steamer *Aldenham* bound for Sydney, and the first mail from the first Australian Imperial Naval and Military Expedition was put aboard, and the vessel resumed her journey after a stay of about half an hour, being cheered on her way by the troops.

The chaplain from H.M.A.S. *Sydney* conducted the Church Parade on the troopship on the Sunday morning, after which the men were free to dispose of the afternoon in any manner they wished. The naval portion of the force were allowed shore leave as they had done such good work in getting the troops ashore during the week, and there were not sufficient boats to take all the troops ashore.

An accident was narrowly averted in the afternoon when the boats were being hauled up to the davits after the return from the island. One boat was being hauled up with two men on the guide ropes when a rope broke and the boat dropped to the water, leaving the men hanging in mid-air. They soon swarmed down the ropes to the boat, which was quickly righted and new ropes fitted. Had the men fallen into the water they stood a good chance of making a dainty morsel for "Jack Shark," who was seen hovering about the vessel on several occasions.

While at Palm Island the opportunity was taken of having target practice. A level spot was picked out at the foot of a high hill and miniature targets erected. Each man was allowed five shots, the scores of each company being totalled and averaged to ascertain which companies had the best shots. The entrenching tools were here brought into use, shallow holes being dug from which the men fired at the targets.

Palm Island is only a few hours steam from Townsville, and at holiday time many people visit Blake's settlement, which is built opposite a sandy beach where there are several bungalows for the accommodation of visitors from the mainland. Whenever possible those men who were financially healthy paid a visit to Blake's dining room about lunch time, when roast veal, fruit salad, apricots, cream, home-made scones, butter and jam, and lettuce could be had for one and sixpence. After the stews for which the *Berrima's* cooks (but not the troops) seemed to have a strange liking, it can readily be imagined that such meals were particularly enjoyable. The men were waited on by Mr. and Mrs. Blake and their sixteen year old son, George, a fine strapping lad over six feet high and broad in proportion, who has been on the island all his life and never worn a pair of boots.

On Monday morning the 31st August, the *Aorangi* arrived and anchored in the bay. The *Aorangi* was being used as a store-ship for the fleet. However, the most important point to the men on the troopship was that this vessel had been used as a mail boat between Sydney and Palm Island. During the day the letters were handed out, but as only one day's notice had been given by the authorities that a mail was being despatched many people were unable to take the opportunity of writing to members of the force, and as the result of a general opinion in Sydney that news of the war would not be passed, only a very few of the men received any newspapers, and those who were the lucky recipients of a paper were much sought after by their comrades. Several papers were pasted up at the top of one of the companion ways on the well deck and the spot was besieged as long as the print could be seen.

A small steamer arrived from Townsville laden with stores, mostly beef, cabbage and potatoes, and all day the men were busily engaged in stowing it down below. Those who had letters written, and those who had the time at their disposal to write letters during the morning, took the opportunity of sending them off by the crew of the *Bobbie Towns* to be posted when they returned to Townsville.

On Wednesday the 2nd September, the early morning parade was at a standstill when a strange object was seen coming from the south. Many wagers were made as to whether it was a submarine or not. At length the little vessel passed close by and moored alongside the *Sydney*. About half an hour later the second of Australia's submarines also moored alongside the *Sydney*. The two submarines were the main subject of talk during the day, it being the first time that many of the men had seen the two "underwater fighting boats," which had been in Australian waters for less than four months.

The fleet had evidently been waiting for the arrival of the submarines before proceeding on the journey northwards as the *Berrima's* boats were all hauled up to the davits and no one sent ashore during the day.

CHAPTER 5

Moving Northwards

At eight bells on the afternoon of Wednesday, 2nd September, a string of flag signals fluttered out from the *Sydney's* mast, and the two submarines cast off from alongside the cruiser. Each of the four vessels weighed anchor and the *Sydney* lead the way out through the northern entrance to the bay. The submarines steamed alongside the *Sydney*, one on either side, while the *Encounter*, *Berrima* and *Aorangi* followed the *Sydney* in single line ahead formation. The *Berrima* had been lying off Palm Island for ten days and everyone on board was glad to be on the move once more.

As the vessels were still steaming along inside the Great Barrier Reef the water was as calm as the proverbial mill pond, and there were no complaints of sea-sickness until 3 p.m. on Thursday (3rd September), when the fleet passed through a very narrow strait into the open sea once more. Parades were in full swing, and as the *Berrima* met the swell the men moved a little in their ranks. "Now, men! Steady! Not a move!" said one officer as the *Berrima* butted into a wave and he lurched across the deck, much to the amusement of the men he was drilling.

During the stay at Palm Island dungaree trousers and shirts, etc., had been issued, and instead of the familiar khaki uniform the men were now garbed in these garments, which had to be worn until further notice. Helmets had also been served out and the regulation felt hat had been stowed away in the kit bags.

There was no canteen on board the troopship, and the want

of soap and various small items was keenly felt by many members of the force who had relied on being able to obtain such articles on the *Berrima*. After the afternoon meal on Friday most of the men took up positions on the boat deck. It had been rumoured that Port Moresby would be the next port of call, while some had it that the fleet was bound for Thursday (Thirsty) Island. About 6 p.m. land was sighted to the eastward and soon afterwards a vessel was seen ahead signalling by searchlight.

In time of peace lights show the narrow entrance through the reef to Port Moresby but since the declaration of war the lights have not been used. Two of the destroyers, inside the entrance, pointed out the way to the incoming vessels, which anchored in the bay about 7.30 p.m. The *Yarra* was just inside the reef and the troops on the *Berrima* cheered heartily as they passed by. Soon after the troopship had come to an anchorage a boat manned by natives, with a couple of officials, was rowed out to ascertain the vessel's name.

Early on Saturday morning the *Sydney* and the *Encounter* moved further up the bay to a basin where they were invisible from seawards. The *Berrima* also moved in soon after daybreak. The *Kanowna*, which had left Townsville with troops for garrison duty at Thursday Island, etc., was in the bay, having been there for three weeks. In addition to the vessels which had arrived the evening before were two oil boats, two colliers, three destroyers and the *Kanowna*—fourteen vessels in all.

Natives soon rowed alongside in their strange craft—*katamarangs*—loaded with cocoanuts and *paw-paws*. Buckets were lowered over the sides of the vessel with money or clothes in them, for which the natives gave their *paw-paws* or cocoanuts. Trading with the natives occupied a good deal of the men's time. Coins were thrown into the water for which the natives dived from their boats, quickly re-appearing with the coins.

So many coins were thrown over that the natives were soon tired of diving for anything but silver. Copper coins were allowed to sink out of sight. The idea was hit upon of covering the copper coins with silver paper. The ruse worked and the natives dived for the seemingly silver coin, re-appearing with the cop-

Scene in native village.

per coin and a piece of silver paper in their hands and a look of annoyance on their faces at having been swindled.

On Saturday afternoon the *Kanowna* was brought alongside the *Berrima*, and when the afternoon parade was concluded at four o'clock the troops of the two States were soon exchanging experiences. The men of the *Kanowna* were not having so good a time as those aboard the *Berrima*. Water was scarce on their boat, and each man received only three pints of fresh water per day for drinking purposes. All washing had to be done in salt water. Some of the fresh beef taken on at Palm Island was transhipped to the *Kanowna*, which moved away again on Sunday morning and again took up her anchorage near the *Encounter*.

While at anchor several men took the opportunity of fishing. There were several lines and hooks but a scarcity of sinkers. However, necessity is the mother of invention, and on Sunday afternoon the fishermen were able to sink their lines by tying pieces of the plum duff the cook had made for Sunday's dinner, just by way of a treat.

A launch from the township, with several residents (including two ladies), came out to the *Berrima* on Sunday afternoon and put aboard several cases of cocoa, milk, matches, etc. When the matches were hoisted up the men cheered lustily and their faces lighted up (but not their cigarettes, for the matches were not issued). Matches had been scarce throughout the voyage and, with cigarettes and tobacco, were at a premium.

On Monday morning the natives were making for the vessels arrayed in all kinds of clothes, a coat of an officer of the R.A.G.A.; some with *lub-lub* and singlet; others with only a *lub-lub* and a string of beads, while not a few had on only the string of beads and a smile, bringing out cocoanuts and *paw-paws* to trade with, but the fleet was on the move before they got alongside. Some of the vessels had left during the night. Once clear of the reef the fleet steamed along in two lines, the *Encounter*, followed by the *Aorangi*, being the starboard line, while the *Sydney*, followed by the *Berrima* and *Kanowna*, formed the other line, and the destroyers *Warrego* and *Yarra* were slipping through the water on the port side of the *Kanowna*.

1. Receiving the mail.   2. Signal Station.

3. A fighting family. Messrs. S. W., A. A. and F. D. Wallace (brothers) with the New Guinea Force.

A small steamer was seen making for Port Moresby from the southward, and a flutter of bunting from the *Sydney* sent the two destroyers racing through the middle of the fleet after the little vessel, with which they soon came up, and after satisfying themselves that all was in order, rejoined the fleet. About midday the *Kanowna*, *Sydney* and the two destroyers dropped behind, the other vessels continuing their course, the *Encounter* taking the lead. The vessels which had dropped behind were soon lost to sight, but by 4 p.m. the *Sydney* and two destroyers took up their former positions. The *Kanowna* had been left behind and ordered back to port owing to some trouble in the engine room.

During Monday night the two submarines joined the fleet, and about 5 p.m. on Tuesday, the *Parramatta*, convoying a collier and an oil tank, were overhauled. There were then eleven vessels in the fleet, but the three which had just been caught up with were soon left behind. Since leaving Port Moresby the troopship had been steaming with all lights out, and as soon as dusk came down the fun used to begin, and men cautiously moved about the decks for fear of falling over ropes, winches, and other gear, or their sleeping comrades.

On Wednesday morning Deal Island was passed, and the troops were somewhat puzzled when it was seen that the fleet was steaming westward off Rossell Island. It soon transpired that the larger vessels had gone round the southern and eastern ends of the island and were steaming westward to meet the three vessels passed the previous evening, which were able to go through channels too shallow for the bigger boats.

About 9 a.m. the whole lay-to off Rossell Island, and a smudge of smoke out on the horizon soon showed itself, coming from the *Australia*, which steamed majestically through the fleet, and lay-to close behind the *Berrima*, while the mails brought from Sydney by the troopship were transferred to the flagship of the Australian fleet. Soon after the flagship joined the fleet another speck was noticed on the horizon in an easterly direction, and several flags were hoisted on the *Australia*.

An answering pennant fluttered from the *Warrego*, which raced away after the approaching vessel, which turned out to be the heavily laden collier *Whairoa*.

The fact of the *Australia* having joined the fleet was evidence that the New Zealand troops had taken possession of the German Samoan Islands. Details were learned later on, and a short account of how those islands were captured will be of interest.

A force of a thousand men left Wellington on August 15th in two troopships—*Moeraki* and *Monowai*—and reached Apia a fortnight later, when the British flag was hoisted without opposition.

The troopships were convoyed by three British cruisers and the *Australia* and *Melbourne*. The fleet first called at Noumea, where the French residents gave the New Zealanders a right royal time. Presents of fruit, chocolates, tobacco, cigarettes, biscuits, etc., were freely given and the Union Jack and the Tricolour were flown side by side on the principal buildings.

On August 23rd the Australian warships and the French cruiser *Montcalm* joined the troopships, and the force was landed at Apia, which was taken without resistance on the 29th August. Pickets were placed in the streets, at buildings and on bridges, and a party was sent off to capture the wireless station.

The next day, August 30th, the troops were lined up, together with residents of many nationalities, and the Union Jack was hoisted to the accompaniment of ringing cheers from the assembled troops, and a formal proclamation read.

The German Governor, Dr. Schulz, was aware of the approaching force, as the high power wireless station that had been erected on the island had tapped conversations between the convoying cruisers, and he stated that the Germans had not intended to offer any resistance.

Had the Imperial Government backed up New Zealand's action thirty years ago, the islands would never have been under German rule. Britain and Germany mutually agreed to recognise Samoa's independence, but when Britain was at war in South Africa in 1899 Germany annexed the islands, notwithstanding the obligations imposed by the "scrap of paper."

At 4.30 p.m., after having lain-to all day, the fleet moved off once more in a westerly direction and met the *Parramatta* and auxiliary vessels passed the previous afternoon. There were now thirteen vessels in the fleet, which was again steaming northwards. During the night a third collier joined the fleet, and on Thursday morning two picturesque, low-lying islands of coral formation, were passed, cocoanut palms coming right down to the white sandy beaches, skirted by coral reefs on which the waves were beating, shooting the spray high into the air.

After passing these islands the fleet divided into three divisions, the *Sydney* and destroyers forged ahead, and were quickly out of sight; the *Encounter* dropped behind to convoy the slower travelling auxiliary vessels. The *Australia* was the only vessel with the troopship, but as the former is a match for any of the enemy vessels in the Pacific nothing was to be feared.

The next morning (Friday, 11th September) the *Australia*, closely followed by the *Berrima*, steamed through St. George's Channel, separating Neu Pommern from Neu Mecklenberg, and round Cape Gazelle. The *Sydney* and destroyers were already lying off Herbertshohe, and signals were being flashed to the flagship.

The first Australian Navy and Military Expedition had reached the enemy's territory at last, having taken twenty-four days to cover the 1,965 miles from Sydney to Herbertshohe.

1. *First Landing at Herbertshohe.*   2. *Bringing wounded on board Berrima in first prize captured.*
3. *Hoisting flag at Herbertshohe.*

CHAPTER 6

Capture of German New Guinea

The *Sydney* and destroyers reached Herbertshohe early on Friday morning, 11th September, 1914, and no time was lost in landing a party under Commander J. A. H. Beresford to destroy the wireless station situated at Bita Paka, about twelve miles inland from Herbertshohe. Landing at the latter place at dawn the town was occupied without opposition and the Union Jack hoisted in the enemy's territory, at 7.30 a.m. By this time the *Australia*, followed by the *Berrima*, had arrived and anchored a short distance off the shore. The men-o'-war looked as if they meant business as they lay-to off the township, with their big guns trained on various points ready to open fire at any moment.

The party of naval reservists transferred to the *Sydney* and destroyers at Port Moresby, which landed with the object of capturing the Bita Paka wireless station, met with opposition soon after leaving the coastline. The fighting all took place within a couple of miles of the wireless station and in the vicinity of Kaba Kaul. Dense tropical vegetation skirted the narrow road on either side, affording admirable opportunities for ambuscades, and had the German forces been in possession of a couple of machine guns the territory would not have passed into British hands as easily as it did.

A few miles on the eastward side of the Bita Paka wireless station, the Germans had entrenched themselves at a bend commanding an uninterrupted view of the road for some distance.

It was here that the party of naval reserves were ambushed.

Fired at from the trench across the road, and from the dense tropical bush on either side the little party gave way not one inch. Courtney, Williams and Pockley went down, but this only made the Australians more determined than ever, and they had no thought of giving in.

Some members of the machine gun section came up with the naval reserves just as they ran into the ambush, but owing to the dense forest on either side of the roadway and the entrenched position of the enemy in front, the machine guns were not brought into use.

This handful of men stuck gamely to their task, and eventually drove the German forces from their position at the point of the bayonet. The natives and Germans who fell at this spot were afterwards buried in the trench that had been dug across the road.

The *Warrego* was the first to hear of the news of the ambuscade, and great praise is due to all the men of the destroyer for the promptitude with which they landed to assist the force on land. Grasping rifles and ammunition they landed, without waiting to put on coats or boots, and lined the road. When the reinforcements, consisting of the balance of the naval reserves and a twelve pounder field gun, were brought up, valuable information was given by the *Warrego's* men, to whom great credit is due for the manner in which they kept the line of communication along a narrow road, with dense tropical bush on either side full of native troops skilled in bushcraft.

Before reaching the first trench mines were passed over, but the connections were incomplete. The missing connections were on their way from Rabaul, and had the Australians reached the spot twenty minutes later the mines would have been fired under them. One of the *Warrego's* men surprised a German officer working on the connections of one mine, and took him prisoner, after first placing him out of action with a shot in the wrist, necessitating an amputation.

The men pushed on and ultimately reached the wireless station at Bita Paka, where several Germans were taken prisoners without loss. These men, though armed, swore that the plant was

1. Captain Pockley (wounded) being brought on board Berrima.

2. Camping after march on Kabu Kaul.

3. Watching native climbing.

owned by a "Private Company," and not by the *Kaiser's* Government. Of course, this didn't go down with the Australian lads, who occupied the station after about eighteen hours strenuous work. The three steel towers which had been got into position for the wireless aerials had been blown down by the Germans on the approach of the invaders.

The permanent buildings were being erected from reinforced concrete on steel framework, and were surrounded by large iron tanks in concrete wells roofed over.

The most important gear was removed to Rabaul and used in connection with the erection of the wireless station at Namanula.

At the time of writing, a start has been made to complete the high power station at Bita Paka, and it is anticipated that it will be in working order about August, 1915.

Although incomplete and working at low power only, it was found that the wireless station, when finished, would have been one of the finest in the Southern Hemisphere. Two large motor cars with trailers had been used to convey all the gear from the coast to the site, which had been admirably chosen from a defensive point of view, being surrounded on three sides by wide steep gullies and on the fourth side was a grassy slope without a vestige of cover for a considerable distance.

On Friday afternoon, the left half battalion of the infantry was landed under Col. Watson, with a view to making a move on Kaba Kaul, where a party of the naval reserves had met with opposition. Shots were exchanged with the enemy's scouts, but as their main body could not be located the order was given to return to Herbertshohe, which was reached about 7 p.m.

The following letter written by one of the men with the expedition gives an interesting account of this march and of his first experiences in the enemy's territory:—

We were informed our force that had been sent to destroy the wireless station at Kaba Kaul met with resistance, and the evidence was soon handed to us by our mortally wounded comrades, Captain Pockley and A.B. Williams, being brought aboard the *Berrima*. As I looked at these

German with collection of native spears and curios.

poor fellows being carried up the gangway I was stirred with emotion. They were heroes, and after silently covering them with all the praise, sympathy and fine feelings I possessed, a terrible clamour for revenge seized me. To wield the bayonet and drive it home with all my might into the murderer of a non-combatant (our Dr. Pockley) was my consummate wish.

Orders were issued for the landing of the left half battalion, with naval gun's crew and machine gun section. We speedily got ashore and commenced our march on to the wireless station. It was a treat to see the naval boys haul their gun over the uneven country—wire fencing and broken-down trees did not deter them. Their stamina was admirable. Shortly before dusk, we reached a branch of the main road leading to Lesson Point and a short cut to the wireless station. We halted here for a few minutes while our scouts were making observations and exchanging compliments with the enemy's scouts.

I won't forget that march. I had two hundred rounds of ammunition, a two-pound tin of jam, tin of bully, biscuits for two days, a camera and films, with a heliograph hanging round my neck to counterbalance the weight at the back. The heat was oppressive. We silently marched back to our base. I was carrying my rifle at the slope, and I thought I would give the left arm a rest; as I took the rifle away I was amazed to find the left arm remained in the same position, so I knocked it down with the rifle and circulation once more continued. Got into Herbertshohe again, and I think I had the best cup of tea I ever tasted. It was just ordinary cheap tea, but in my condition it was a 'gift of the Gods.'

We quartered at the Post Office for the night, and I will always smile when I think of it. I took up my watch at the signal station at 10.30 p.m. About 11.30 I moved about twenty yards from the station and was standing beside a tree, when *Bang! Ping!* No place for an honest man with a sentry like that. I dropped on all fours and got back to my

Native prisoners brought into Rabaul from the hills.

Native Prisoners.

post. I was relieved at 12.30 a.m., and having made myself comfortable, soon fell asleep. I was rudely awakened by volley after volley and movements of my comrades getting on the alert.

Our N.C.O. struggled manfully into his equipment, seized his rifle and sat down. 'Where's my boots?' 'That's *my* rifle.' 'Fall in! The Germans are here, boys?' 'Steady there, lads,' came from an old South African campaigner who was quietly cuddling his rifle and lighting his pipe behind a box. 'Get your rifles handy,' while the groans and expressions from another old soldier rivetted my attention for a minute. A young Australian lad—a trainee—got a little excited in his haste to get his 'fighting kit' together, and in the dark walked not too kindly on the stomach of this old Imperial soldier, who had a great record and was number 13. His language was quite expressive of his feelings, and very decisive.

No. 13 had had other misfortunes. He fell down the hatch of the *Berrima*; fell over a cliff on Mount Mother, and only saved himself from certain destruction by grasping a rock; he was hauled up with a rope and was quite exhausted; he banged his head against a tree on Palm Island, which left a nasty scar. He confidentially informed me he did not expect to return from this expedition, but that it didn't matter. He got home alright though.

It was a relief to find that the alarm was false. The enemy was not at hand, so I soon dropped off to sleep again. I was up early and having a look round, when to my dismay I saw a poor pig with an ugly gash in his shoulder, unmistakably a bayonet wound. It was quite evident the poor fellow was having a walk and came on a sentry who halted him, but not understanding our language, continued his advance, was shot at, missed, and then bayonetted. He was shot at dawn. The troops had pork for breakfast.

Although the officer commanding the German forces defending the wireless station at Bita Paka had surrendered, there was still a large force of German and native troops in the field,

45

1. *Herbertshöhe Post Office.*   2. *Drawing water at Herbertshöhe.*   3. *Naval gun's crew.*

so having dismantled the Bita Paka wireless station, and placed a garrison at Herbertshohe, the fleet steamed into Simpsonshafen, on which stands Rabaul, the capital of the German Pacific possessions.

The *Berrima* steamed into Simpsonshafen about four o'clock, passed the Australian warships lying at anchor in the bay with guns ready for instant action

The troopship went alongside the thousand-foot jetty of the N.D.L. Co., and 600 troops (500 infantry and 100 naval), under the command of Col. Paton, landed at dark on the evening of 12th September, 1914, with only one accident—Private Hoskins slipped on the gangway, sustaining injuries to the leg which laid him up for a fortnight.

Apart from some desultory firing which took place between the advance guards and the enemy on the hills, north and east of Rabaul, no opposition was met with.

One company marched out to occupy Namanula, a native police boy being shot for not obeying the command to halt. Although Namanula is only two miles from Rabaul it was not reached until the next morning.

A month previously the seat of government had been transferred from Rabaul to Toma, several miles inland, between Rabaul and Herbertshohe. The governor with his officials, and the remainder of the military forces had also moved to Toma.

At daybreak on Monday, 14th September, the *Encounter* shelled the ridges in the direction of Toma for half an hour, and Colonel Watson left Herbertshohe at 5 a.m. in command of four companies of infantry, a machine gun section, and a twelve-pounder field gun, reaching Toma without opposition about three o'clock in the afternoon.

Dr. Haber, the Deputy-Governor of New Guinea and Brigadier Holmes of the British force met at Herbertshohe on Tuesday to discuss terms and conditions of capitulation, and the German and native forces surrendered at Herbertshohe on the 21st September, 1914.

Following are the names of those killed and wounded in the fighting around Herbertshohe:—

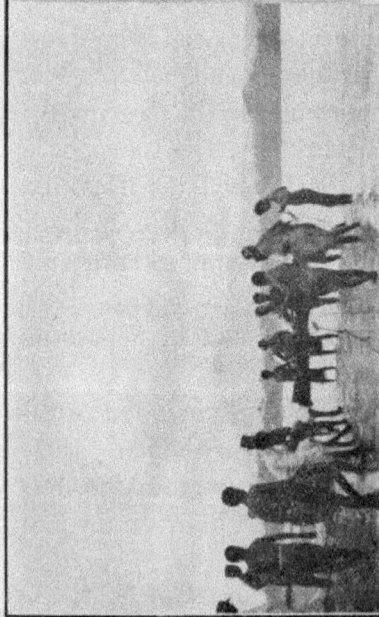

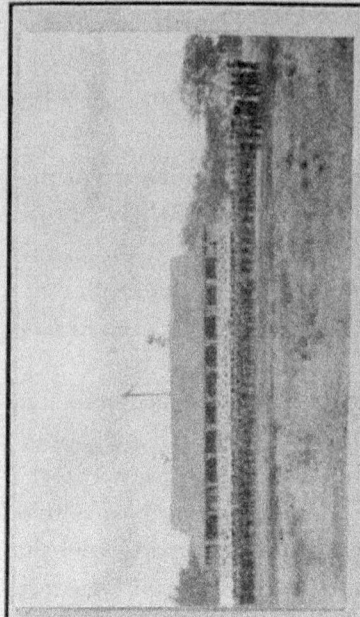

1. Natives fishing at Rabaul.
2. Hospital at Namanula. Mt. Mother in distance.
3. Troops at Garrison Headquarters.
4. Crossing between Matupi Island and the mainland.

Killed.

Lieut.-Commander Chas. B. Elwell.

Capt. Brian Coldham Antill Pockley, of the A.M.C.

Wm. G. V. Williams, able seaman, No. 4 Company Naval Reserves.

John Courtney, able seaman, No. 3. Company Naval Reserves.

—— Street, able seaman, No. 6 Company Naval Reserves.

Wounded.

Robt. Moffatt, able seaman, No. 3 Company Naval Reserves; who subsequently died on H.M.A.S. *Sydney* and was buried at sea.

Daniel Skillen, able seaman, No. 3 Company Naval Reserves.

T. Sullivan, able seaman, No. 6 Company Naval Reserves.

J. Tonks, able seaman, No. 6 Company Naval Reserves.

On Sunday afternoon, 13th September, 1914, the troops and naval detachment, residents and native police were drawn up on a vacant piece of ground—now known as Proclamation Square—where a flagpole had been erected, and at 3 p.m. the Union Jack was broken by Lieutenant Basil Holmes, A.D.C., and saluted by all present. The flagship of the Australian Navy fired a Royal salute, after which the National Anthem was sung— the *Australia's* band supplying the music. Three rousing British cheers were then given for " His Majesty King George V."

The proclamation issued by the brigadier was read by the Brigade Major, F. B. Heritage, and as the troops marched past, the flag was again saluted.

A proclamation was then read to the natives and police boys, who also gave three cheers for their new king.

Copies of these proclamations are given in Chapter 14.

1. Native Police Boy.   2. Kanaka Boy.   3. Street Scene, Rabaul.

CHAPTER 7

Australia's First Naval Loss— Submarine "AE" 1

A few days after the capture of the German Pacific possessions by the Australian force, submarine *AE*. 1 was lost with all
hands. The actual circumstances surrounding her loss will prob-
ably never be known, but that it was the result of an accident
there can be no doubt. The last that was seen of her was at 3.30
p.m. on September 14th, when returning to Simpsonhafen from
patrol duty. No enemy ships were in the vicinity, and the ocean
around was as calm as the proverbial mill pond—much calmer
than the weather the little craft had encountered on her world
famous voyage from England to Australia in company with her
sister ship the *AE*. 2, convoyed by the *Sydney*.

Australia's first two submarines had become quite a familiar
object to the members of the Expedition, having accompanied
the fleet from Palm Island to the capital of the Bismarck Archipelago, cutting through the waves alongside the larger vessels
of the fleet, or out ahead ready to meet the enemy should he
venture in sight.

Although the loss was not brought about by any action of
the enemy, thirty-five officers and men gave their lives to the
Empire just as truly as if they had been killed in an encounter
with the enemy.

The water in the vicinity of where the *AE*. 1 was last seen is
very deep, and if that is where the little vessel sank, death would

have come suddenly, as the sides of the vessel would not have been able to withstand the great pressure.

Australia's first submarine was manned by the majority of the officers and men who had brought her safely through her long voyage from England, and the names of those thirty-five men are here given:—

Lieut.-Commander Thomas F. Besant, lent to the Royal Australian Navy by the Admiralty (was spoken of as a specialist in submarine work).

Lieut. Hon. Leopold Scarlett.

Lieut. C. L. Moore.

Petty Officers.—Robert Smail, Henry Hodge, William Tribe, Thomas Guilbert.

Leading Seaman.—G. Corbould.

Seamen.—John Reardon, S. W .Worland, Jack Jarman, James B. Thomas, A. H. Fisher, Fred. Dennis, George Hodgkin.

Signalman.—George Dance.

Telegraphist.—Cyril L. Baker.

Artificers.—Thomas F. Lowe, J. A. Marsland, J. W. Wilson, J. A. Fettes, John Messenger. Chief Stoker.—Harry Stretch.

Stoker Petty Officers.—John J. Maloney, Charles F. Wright, William Waddylove.

Leading Stokers.—S. C. Barton, J. Meek, William Guy.

Stokers.— P. L. Wilson, J. J. Bray, Ernest Blake, R. B. Holt, James Guild, H. J. Gould.

The submarines *AE* 1 and *AE* 2 entered Port Jackson on Sunday morning, 24th May, 1914, having accomplished the longest voyage that had ever been attempted by such craft— over twelve thousand miles—without serious mishap. Launched at Vicker's Yards on 21st May, 1913, the two submarines were commissioned at Portsmouth on 28th February, 1914.

126 feet in length by 22½ feet, and with a displacement of

800 tons; their 1,600 H.P. Diesel oil engines (a German invention by the way) are capable of driving the "underwater" boats at sixteen knots on the surface, while the electric motors move them along under the water at ten knots per hour.

Armed with four torpedo tubes, and with guns on disappearing mountings, the submarines of the *AE* class were likely to make short work of any ships that might be met flying the enemy flag.

The British Empire generally—Australia in particular—mourns the loss of her gallant sons.

> *Our Lost Submarine.*
> *Australians mourn. Your sons have gone;*
> *They sank beneath the wave,*
> *All bottled up within a shell*
> *They've gone into their grave.*
> *Just weep and pray for those brave lads,*
> *Those lads in navy blue,*
> *Who for Australia gave their lives,*
> *Lives of Lads so true.*
>
> *AE 1 submarine has sunk;*
> *She's gone beneath the tide,*
> *Ne'er sight of her again we'll see*
> *Upon those waters wide.*
> *She patrolled o'er the ocean blue*
> *Attached to our good fleet,*
> *Her crew were watching for the foe*
> *Expecting them to meet.*
>
> *With eyes alert, each at his post,*
> *No thought of danger near,*
> *For they who work within those shells*
> *Know not the word of fear.*
> *A cruel blow to those on board—*
> *Much worse for some on shore,*
> *For mothers now will miss their sons;*
> *Miss them all for evermore.*

CHAPTER 8

Mt. Mother and Her Daughters; Matupi Island and Sulphur Springs

Towering 2,270 feet above Rabaul on the eastern, or seaward side, is Mount Mother, with her daughter only a hundred yards away, while on the northern side towers her North Daughter. Away to the south, beyond Matupi Island, is the South Daughter, hidden from Rabaul by a large extinct crater, near the foot of which is another large extinct crater with a smaller semi-active one inside.

The summit of Mount Mother is distant about seven miles from Rabaul, *via* Namanula, through the hospital grounds, and then by a narrow native track only a foot wide.

Being the most prominent spot round Rabaul, the summit of Mount Mother was eagerly scanned through glasses as soon as the Australians landed at Rabaul, and it was seen that the enemy was in occupation. Just below the sky-line were a couple of small tents, and several figures appeared to be engaged in digging trenches.

It was decided to send out a small force of men to reconnoitre, and ascertain the strength of the enemy. On the Monday afternoon after landing, a section of "D" Company, under the command of Lieut. McDowell, set out for the purpose of gaining this information.

After leaving the hospital the little party passed over several steep gullies, then through Kanaka plantations, where there were

Mount Mother from Namanula.

bananas, cocoanuts and *paw-paws*. For a few miles they cautiously made their way through these plantations along the narrow
track, where a false step meant rolling some hundreds of feet
down the steep sides of the gullies on either side.

The hardest part of the climb was over the last two miles up
the side of the mountain—the steepest part—where there was
not a single tree that could be used as cover or even as protection against the blasting rays of "Old Sol."

However, nothing daunted, they pushed on and reached the
summit just on dusk. Hurried investigations showed that Germans had been camped there and had begun several trenches,
but, as at other points, they had been surprised ere they had
time to complete arrangements for the defence of their strategic
positions.

On the seaward side of the mountain a hut had been built,
and this was well stocked with tinned provisions for the German
signallers stationed there, but who had made good their retreat.
The tinned goods were handed round and sampled. As the la-
bels were in German, this was the only manner of ascertaining
what was inside the tins, and it was amusing to note the look of
satisfaction, or otherwise, as the men sampled such items as "pre-
served fruit, bacon, fish, knife polish, *sauerkraut*, black bread, etc.

Camping in the hut for the night—it was fired in the morning—a stupid action, as it would have been of inestimable value
to the men who were afterwards stationed on the mountain to
watch for any vessels approaching the port.

A letter written by a member of the expedition, who was
stationed at Mount Mother for eleven weeks, is full of interest
and is here given:—

I got to the top of Mount Mother after a three hours
arduous climb. A signal station was formed and communication with Rabaul and Herbertshohe established.
The Mother is 2,500 feet above sea level, and one of the
healthiest spots on the island. We pitched our tent during
a terrific storm, and we afterwards found it was a continuous storm, always blowing, except in the rainy season,
when the monsoons paid a regular visit.

Sulphur Creek, near Rabaul.

The first week brought the tent down. It fell in a gale at night when we had all turned in. The tent pole luckily missed my head, but fell across my chest. We could not put it up again that night, so we went to a shelter built of bamboos and German waterproof sheets and used for the lookout, intending to stay there for the night, but it only lasted against the storm for a couple of hours longer and was lifted bodily out of the ground. We had a long, miserable wait till morning to re-pitch our tent.

This was not the worst I had to put up with. There were rats in hundreds on the mountain. It was almost impossible to sleep. At night their day started. They held race meetings round the tent in the early part of the night 2nd when everything was quiet, they came inside and jumped over our bodies. They liked the human skin for food. One of the boys was bitten on the toe; one awakened to find Mr. Rat gnawing the hard skin on the soles of his feet.

Their favourite game was to tickle our faces with their whiskers. Boots, bayonets, and even revolvers were used, but no death occurred. Hitting on a good plan we killed twenty-six the first night. A half-filled bucket of water, with bread in it, brought them along. Gangways were made for them from the ground to the buckets with pieces of bread, and they 'fell in.'

Snakes in plenty showed great familiarity. They came into the tent and generally made themselves at home, except when we introduced the bayonet. Then the monsoons came along, and with them myriads of insects and flies. The wind and rain were deafening, beating against our tent. We had to dig trenches through the tent, the rain was so heavy. The calm brought the insects, which were almost unbearable. They got all over us—in our hair, down our backs. Our tea was turned into soup. Ants were the only insects I could distinguish amongst the number. We ate insects with every meal.

Great was our relief after eleven weeks of this life. The Germans wondered how we stuck to it; they never did more than three or four days without illness.

The wind blew all our plates and pannikins away, and so boisterous was it one night that our iron dixy was blown down the side of the mountain, being recovered next morning after three hours search by two natives.

On the whole, our stay was enjoyable. I look back on it and it gives me pleasure to think I have seen a few more little bits of life.

At the eastern entrance to Simpsonshaven is Matupi Island, where there is a very large native settlement. It is on this island that the German Government erected large sheds for storing coal for their Pacific fleet; on the further shores of Matupi Harbour are targets were the *Scharnhorst* and *Gneisenau* indulged in practice.

Matupi Island is only a few feet above sea level in the highest part, and whenever the volcanoes are at all wakeful the island quakes from end to end. For some time prior to the rainy season earthquakes are of frequent occurrence. During the time the troops were at Rabaul several earthquakes were felt, the largest being at 7.23 p.m. on October 19th, lasting for over a minute, and all the buildings (all weatherboard, fortunately) rocked and shook from side to side. Several hundreds of tons of rock and soil were displaced in the crater near Matupi.

Opposite Matupi Island, in the entrance to Rabaul Harbour, are two high rocky islets resembling in appearance enormous beehives. Beyond them is Vulkan Island, which came into existence in a single night, when the craters were busy about forty years ago.

In the crevices on the sides of the craters are large deposits of sulphur, while at the foot of the crater are many hot sulphur springs, the water running into Matupi Harbour. Meals can be cooked here without the aid of a fire by simply putting the viands in tins and leaving them in the boiling water.

The North Daughter, about two miles from Rabaul, rises about 1,800 feet above the town. On the very top of this mountain is a small native settlement surrounded by plantations of corn, cocoanuts, *paw-paws*, etc. It was on this mountain that a

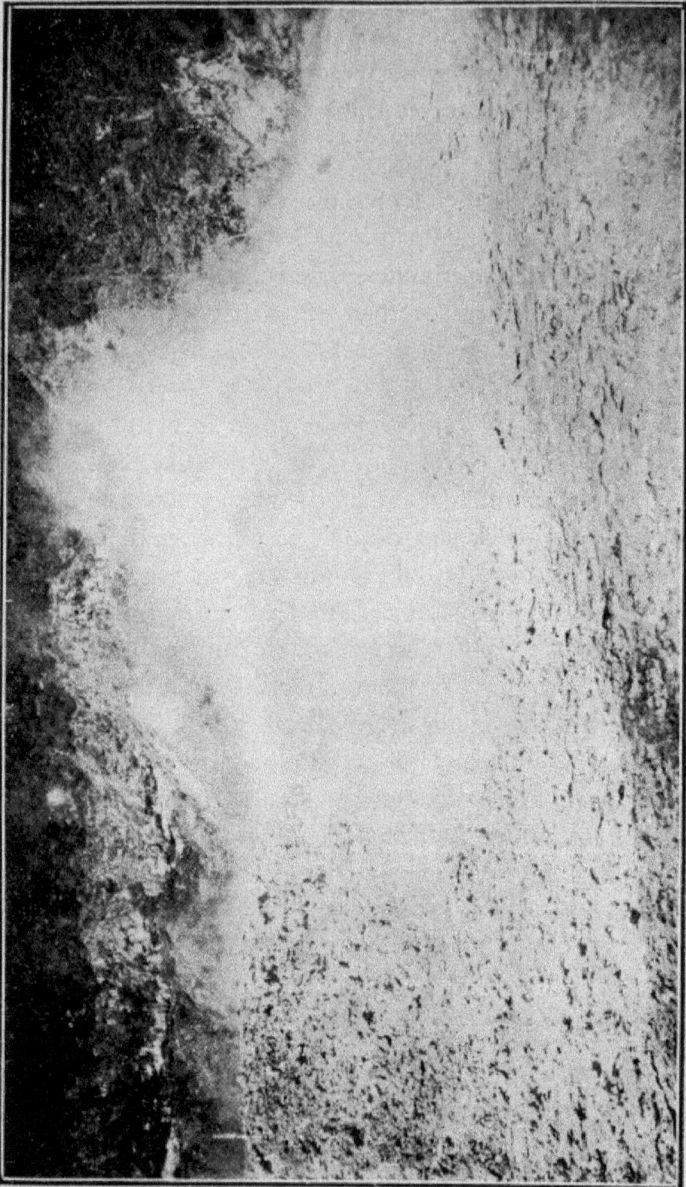

Utopia Crater in eruption.

party of German signallers were stationed when the Australians landed and took possession of the territory on the 12th September, 1914.

Interior of Utopia Crater.

CHAPTER 9

Capture of "Komet" and Other Prizes

The prizes captured by the members of the first Australian Naval and Military Expedition were fairly numerous and of considerable value. Most of the prizes captured were put into commission and used for the transport of troops to various outlying posts, and for trading and communication purposes.

The first captures at Herbertshohe were a couple of motor schooners, which were used in connection with the landing of the troops at that place and also when bringing the wounded men and German prisoners on board the *Berrima*.

The most important and valuable capture, however, was that of K.G.S. *Komet*, which was taken about 170 miles W.S.W. of Rabaul, on the west coast of the island.

The wireless station which had been erected at Namanula, and vessels in the Rabaul Harbour had intercepted messages giving the disposition and number of troops at Rabaul and Herbertshohe, and also the details of the fighting that had taken place at Bita Paka. The officer in charge of the wireless station at Namanula, Lieut. Creswell, was of the opinion that the sending station had been hurriedly erected and was most likely a plant dismantled from some vessel and temporarily erected on shore, as the only wireless station known to be in existence on the island (at Bita Paka) had been captured.

The destroyers were sent off to make a search for any vessels

A few of the prizes captured at Rabaul by the Navy and Naval Reserve.

that might be in hiding along the coast, but without result. The fleet left Rabaul on the 4th October. The larger German men-o'-war, *Scharnhorst*, *Gneisenau*, etc. were playing a game of "hide and seek" in the Pacific, the Australian, Japanese, and French vessels doing all the " seeking."

Provisions for both troops, residents and natives were running low, and should anything happen to the steamer *Moresby*, which had already left Sydney with stores, the question of rations would be a serious one indeed.

From information received from natives it was learned that a vessel was lying in a small secluded harbour a couple of hundred miles from Rabaul on the western coast, and it appeared likely that this was the source of the wireless messages that had been intercepted.

As it was more than probable that this vessel was either the *Komet* or *Planet*, and while it was flying the German ensign, would prove a continual menace to merchant shipping carrying stores for the garrisons, it was decided to despatch an expedition to effect the capture of the vessel and put the wireless plant out of action.

With this object in view, the small steam yacht of the late German governor, fitted with wireless, was armed with a four-pounder in the bows and a twelve-pounder aft. A force for thirty members of the Rabaul garrison, under Col. Paton, and comprising machine gun section, naval gun's crews, and half a dozen members of the infantry was placed on board the *Nusa*, which was put in command of Lieut.-Commander Jackson.

The infantry was for the purpose of capturing the wireless plant, which it was thought would be found on the shore, for while the little seventy-ton *Nusa* attended to the vessel it would be necessary for a land party to effect the capture of the wireless plant.

The *Nusa* left Rabaul early on the 8th October, and making a careful search along the coast reached within a few miles of where the vessel was said to be in hiding. The *Nusa* dropped anchor close to a small island on which a party was landed and the natives interrogated. It was learned from the natives that there

H.M.A.S. Nusa alongside her capture, K.G.S. Komet, now H.M.A.S. Una.   The Nusa was under the command of Commander Jackson, with Colonel Paton in charge of an infantry force.

was a "boat belong fight, he no long way," and also that one of the officers of the vessel had been on the island only that morning shooting pigeons. Sentries were placed round the island so as to prevent the natives leaving in their canoes and warning the enemy of the position of the *Nusa*.

At dawn next morning, with the help of a thick mist, the *Nusa* steamed slowly along the coast into a small harbour not shown on the charts, where the prize was peacefully lying at anchor. With the guns trained on the enemy craft, the *Nusa* got close to the vessel and a boat was lowered, and Col. Paton went aboard without any opposition.

Capt. Muller of the K.G.S. *Komet* (for such was the vessel), who had just arisen, encountered the commanding officer of the expedition (Col. Paton), who demanded the surrender of the vessel. No other action was open to the captain, and his surprise and dismay at seeing his vessel captured so easily by the British forces can be better imagined than described. So keenly did he feel his position that he simply cried. "I was taken quite unawares," he said, "had I seen the little *Nusa* coming she would have been under the water now."

The infantry and machine gun section of the expedition were placed on the *Komet*, which left Talusia at daybreak on the 12th October, reaching Rabaul about 10 a.m. on Tuesday, 13th October. The signal station on Mount Mother reported about 8 a.m. that the *Nusa* was approaching the harbour with the larger gunboat following. There was great excitement in the garrison when the prize was brought into the harbour.

The *Komet*, which left for Sydney on the 17th October, flying the white ensign of the British navy, was fitted with 4-inch guns and put into commission as the *Una*, in charge of Lieut.-Commander Jackson.

Other captures, though not so valuable as the *Komet*, include the steamers *Meklong*, *Sumatra*, *Siar*, and *Madang* (the Herbertshohe mail boat), which vessels have been used constantly since their capture.

The *Madang* was steaming into Herbertshohe with several German reservists on board a few days after the occupation of the territory by the Australians. The *Protector* was lying off the shore and promptly fired a shot across her bows. Too late the *Madang's* officers saw the white ensign of the British navy and endeavoured to make oft, but a second shot from the *Protector* brought home to those on board the *Madang* the futility of attempting to escape.

Several motor schooners were captured, amongst them being the *Samoa*, a fine three-masted vessel of 260 tons, driven by 110 h.p. motor engines, captured by the *Madang* on 25th November in Kalibi Bay, New Ireland. The motor schooners *Matupi* and *Senta*, were discovered in hiding at Tekereki Harbour, New Ireland, and several smaller motor schooners and launches were also captured.

CHAPTER 10

Expeditions to Outlying Islands

The first and largest expedition after reaching Rabaul was to Wilhelmshaven in German New Guinea proper. The *Berrima*, with half the battalion of infantry, machine gun section and naval reserves, left Rabaul on 22nd September at 10 a.m., convoyed by the *Australia, Sydney* and *Encounter* and the French cruiser *Montcalm*.

Wilhelmshaven was reached two days later and occupied without opposition, the Union Jack being hoisted in place of the German Ensign. Seventeen German residents were taken prisoners, but as they all took the oath of neutrality, they were released.

A garrison force of one and a half companies of infantry and half a company of navel reserves were left at Wilhelmshaven, and the fleet steamed away in the afternoon of the same day, reaching Rabaul on the 26th September.

Wilhelmshaven is a very pretty spot but exceedingly unhealthy. Of the two hundred odd men who did garrison duty at that town there was hardly a man who was not down with the fever. The men of this garrison were the first to be relieved and returned home to Sydney.

A wireless station was erected by the officer-in-charge of the garrison—Major Martin—and communication was established with Port Moresby.

On the 16th October the *Nusa*, familiarly called the *Cock-o'-the-North*, and the *Tom Thum,* left Rabaul for the purpose of hoisting the British flag at Kawieang and effecting the release of Mr. Jolley, the British vice-consul, who had been made a prisoner by the Germans on the outbreak of the war, because he would not give his parole.

The expedition was successful in every way. Mr. Jolley was released and taken back to Rabaul. The German commissioner, treasurer, and a reservist were taken as prisoners of war. Information was received that a small steamer, the *Siar*, engaged in smuggling supplies in for German residents, was hiding in Tekereki Harbour, and the *Nusa* was headed in that direction, discovering the *Siar*, and also two large auxiliary motor schooners, the *Matupi* and *Senta*.

The engines of the *Siar* were defective, so she was towed along to Kawieang by the *Nusa*, where she was left in the hands of Petty Officer Clark to be fixed up and brought into Rabaul later on. The *Nusa* left Kawieang again for Rabaul on the 21st October, towing the schooner *Matupi* and with the *Senta* under her own power. Rabaul was reached on the 23rd.

Lieut. Basil Holmes was left in charge of the garrison at Kawieang, and a permanent garrison was despatched from Rabaul by the *Meklong* on the 28th October.

The same day the *Messina*, with 50 troops from "B" Company, a machine gun section and a detachment of the A.M.C., with the administrator and Captain Travers, left for the purpose of occupying Nauru, a small island right on the equator.

On the 3rd November Ocean Island was reached, only 160 miles from Nauru. Both of these islands contain valuable deposits of phosphates, the development of which is being carried out by the Pacific Phosphates Company.

It was found that the Germans had deported about forty employees of the company from Nauru to Ocean Island. It was decided to take these people back to Nauru on the *Messina*.

Leaving Ocean Island on the 5th November, Nauru was reached next day at daylight and, landing under a flag of truce, Captain Travers brought the Resident Commissioner on board the *Messina*. No resistance was offered by the Germans, who were all arrested and taken on board.

The *Messina* left Nauru on the 8th October, reaching Rabaul three days later.

Here is an interesting letter written by a member of the expedition:—

Nauru was the treat of my life. We had to land in rowing boats, and a dozen men could hold the island against an invasion. We landed at daylight, and the Germans who were there got the surprise of their lives. H.M.A.S. *Melbourne* had been there before and hoisted the Union Jack, and when our men left the Germans tore down the flag, burned it, and held a mock funeral over it. A young English woman who was living on the island was insulted and almost assaulted by the Germans. Her husband was away on business, and all other British subjects were sent off from the island or held prisoners.

The three ringing cheers of the lads when the flag was hoisted wakened the Germans and brought forth our insulted sister, who almost got hysterical with delight. She said, 'Thank God! The boys in brown have come.' We gave her three of our best cheers, and arrested the two Germans who had maltreated her. Our officer ordered them to be shot, and only for the intervention of one of the staff officers who had just come ashore they surely would be 'out and under.' Only sixty-two men volunteered to shoot them. Our party numbered sixty-two.

I believe they each got ten years penal servitude.

The estimated value of the island is ninety-four millions sterling. It has the richest deposits of phosphate in the world, and the copra trade is very considerable.

The island has about fourteen miles of coastline, a lagoon in the centre, and tapers gracefully to a summit. Of coral formation, there are countless caves where beautiful cool bathing pools exist.

A party of the infantry, under the command of Major Heritage and Captain Travers, left Rabaul on the *Siar* on the 19th

November for the occupation of the Admiralty Islands.

The islands were reached without mishap, the proclamation issued and the British flag hoisted, the party arriving back at Rabaul on the 30th November.

The head of the Methodist Mission in the Bismarck Archipelago, Rev. Mr. Cox, was thrashed and ill-treated by certain German residents at Namatanai, on the east coast of New Ireland. For the purpose of bringing the lawbreakers to task, Major Ralston, with Lieut. Bruce and 56 men of "G" Company, left Rabaul on Sunday the 9th November. The vessel pulled out from the wharf about four o'clock in the afternoon, without taking her despatches. The *Nusa* was just coming in from Herbertshohe when the despatches were noticed.

Then began a race after the slower travelling *Madang*, the little *Nusa* being given every ounce of steam by her engineer (A. W. Eccleston). The direction of the wind prevented the *Nusa's* whistle being heard, and the *Madang* kept on her course. The little *Nusa* managed about thirteen knots, but the *Madang* had a clear start of an hour, and it was half-past six before the despatches were handed over to the *Madang's* commander.

A couple of hours later, when fairly out to sea, the *Madang* began taking in water, and as the position was likely to become serious, it was decided to put back to Rabaul, which was reached about midnight. The men, with their gear and stores, were transferred to the larger steamer, *Meklong*, which left Simpsonshaven on Tuesday, 11th November.

The expedition was successful in capturing the offenders at Namatanai. Dr. Braunert, the principal in the assault, was captured by Private Watriama. Watriama, who is the rightful king of the Loyalty Islands, fought with the British forces in New Guinea, and wears on his breast the colours of the South African war.

The Loyalty Islands are a French Protectorate, but as Watriama favours the British Government, his brother, who is a strong adherent to French rule, is recognised by the French Government as the king of the Loyalty Islands.

Watriama speaks perfect English, and made himself a favourite with all members of the expedition.

The five Germans captured at Namatanai were brought to Rabaul, tried by court-martial, found guilty, and punishment was inflicted in the presence of the whole of the troops of the Rabaul and Herbertshohe garrisons on the 23rd November, and sent to Sydney by the *Matunga*, which left the same day.

The last expedition was despatched by the *Meklong* on the 5th December, for the purpose of occupying the German Solomon Islands, hoisting the Union Jack thereon and issuing a proclamation. It was thought that a few Germans, with a large force of natives, had entrenched themselves in the hills and a scrap was expected. Two hundred and fifty men of "F," "G," and "H" Companies, together with a machine gun section and the A.M.C. went on board the *Meklong*, under the command of Col. W. R. Watson, Kieta was reached about noon on the 9th December, but as at other parts, no opposition was met with, a white flag having already been hoisted on the Commissioner's residence when Lieut. Holmes went ashore.

Half of "F" Company, under command of Lieut. Maughan, was landed for garrison duty.

It was ascertained at Kieta that a government steamer, the *Buka*, had been sunk there by the Germans about three weeks before the arrival of the expedition.

Although the best position was chosen for camping, and every precaution taken, very few men escaped an attack of fever, and these men were amongst the first to be relieved and returned to Sydney.

The report that the German cruisers had landed a large party in New Guinea, not many miles from Wilhelmshaven, was the cause of the hurried departure of the *Nusa* from Rabaul on December 8th. A number of naval reserves were picked up at Herbertshohe, and in company with the *Elax* (oil boat) and *Yarra*, the *Nusa* set a course for Wilhelmshaven.

With 72 persons on board, the little yacht bore a great similarity to a Sydney tramcar during business hours. There was standing room only.

Trouble was met with soon after leaving Herbertshohe, when something went wrong with the engines. A line was passed from the *Yarra* and the *Nusa* towed, for several hours. The defect was at length fixed up, and the discomforts of the trip were relieved when Wilhelmshaven was reached and half of the men landed.

Then, in company with the *Warrego* and *Yarra*, H.M.A.S. *Nusa*—for she was now properly commissioned, and flying the white ensign of the Royal Navy—steamed along the coast and up the Kaiserin Augusta River in search of the reported German forces. The *Nusa* led the way up the river, owing to her lighter draught, and leaving the *Warrego* some distance up the river, continued the search for a hundred miles further by herself. Needless to say, all hands were continually on the alert, as they had cannibals to deal with as well as Germans. The expedition returned without having encountered the enemy, bringing with them one German trader, who had been taken prisoner many miles up the river.

CHAPTER 11

Native Customs and Habits

The dark members of the human race found at Rabaul include natives of most islands in the Pacific. They rarely work for a master on their own island—only when there is a famine, or when they want money for some purpose.

The boys (they are all "Boys" or "Marys," irrespective of age) usually receive about five marks a moon (month). The Native Police boys represent New Guinea proper, Samoa, various islands of the Solomon group, Carolines, etc., and are all known by the locality they hail from. There are New Guinea boys, those from the Solomons are Solomonny boys, etc. Of course, the Police Boys are of the finest stature, and dealings with them showed that they were of a higher intellect than the native of New Britain, as shown in the making of native mats, canoes, weapons, houses, etc.

The dress of the native is usually a *lub-lub*—a yard or so of gaudy coloured print—with a singlet on special occasions. The kanaka (or native) of New Britain, through coming in contact with many white men, missionaries, traders, etc., has developed keen business methods, and knows the value of his produce and what he should receive in exchange for it. If he is offered more and receives it, all the better for him; he takes the extra, does his best to get the same value next time and tells all his friends.

Although there are natives from so many islands, each with a different dialect, and Chinese, Japanese, Malays, Tongans, Indians, Germans and British, all converse in pidgin English.

The language of the Kanaka contains roughly about two hundred words only, although many German and English words have been picked up from traders and added to their vocabulary. In many cases their method of expression is rather humorous. For instance, a motorcar is spoken of as a "Pinnace-belong-bush"; a man-o'-war is a "boat-belong-fight"; a piano is "big feller box; Missus cross him too much; he plenty cry."

In trading with the natives from outlying villages, the usual question asked by the troops was "What you got?" If their trading was finished, their answer was "Yes, me no got somedin," or "No got," with a shrug of the shoulders and a lifting of the eyebrows. A question frequently put to a native was "You savvy, speakem English," and a few of the troops received a shock in getting the answer "Yes, I understand English as good as you." Enquiries generally discovered the fact that he had been in some British town—usually Sydney—for several years.

A couple of days before each full moon, the natives dress themselves up in the evenings with feathers, leaves, etc., and put bright coloured powders on the face and hair. *Tom-toms* are brought out, together with other noisy native instruments manufactured from reeds and bamboos, and until the "small feller sun" sets the natives keep up their dancing and chanting. Each dance usually lasts about an hour. Moving round the orchestra, the dancers assume grotesque positions, accompanied by weird chantings which can be heard a long way off.

At the big "*sing-sings*" several groups of natives sometimes dance at the one time. All the dances are very much alike to the white man; to the native they are full of variation. It becomes monotonous to watch them. The most interesting is the war dance. A couple of natives, with a cocoanut palm leaf fore and aft, jump round and round, to the accompaniment of the *Boom! Boom! Boom!* of the *tom-tom*, whirling spears above their heads.

At the invitation of the Rev. Mr. Cox a number of the troops visited the Duke of York Islands and saw the Christmas sing-sing. Part of the dress of one native was composed of strips of the Sydney *Daily Telegraph*.

A native feast was prepared for the boys. Pig, fowls, yams,

Native Dance (Duk-duk).

Native Dance (Sing-sing).

Native Dances (Sing-sing). 1 and 2. Ladies' dances.

Sing-sing at Matupi Island, held on Christmas Day.

Native's method of publishing his engagement.

His castle and his Sunday clothes, put on specially for this photograph.

1. Native houses. 2. Native canoe (catamaran). 3. Native house and plantation.

Latest fashions in head-dress.

Group of " Marys" in native attire.

Cocoanut Plantation and Bungalow, Rabaul.

sweet potatoes, and corn were placed in baskets. These were put in a hole in the ground, from which a fire had been taken. The food was then covered with leaves and the burning ashes heaped on top. The cooking result was excellent, as the viands were partaken of with great relish by the troops.

At the conclusion of the *sing-sing*, the boys in khaki got together and sang "The Old Church Choir," "Tipperary," and the National Anthem, while "D" Company's comedian, K. A. Higgins (better known at Harry Lauder), contributed "The Weddin' o' Sandy McNab," much to the amusement of all present. During the first verse, the natives were interested, the second verse caused them to smile a little, but the antics of the little Scotchman in the third verse fairly doubled them up with laughter.

Bidding "*Yorkor*" to their hosts the *Litia* started on her homeward trip to Rabaul at 6 p.m., and a four hours' run brought a pleasant and instructive day's outing to a close.

As with all Christian races, Christmas is made by these people the occasion for holding great "*sing-sings*" and feasts. For days before Christmas the native works for money wherever he can get an employer. Pigs and fowls are looked after and fattened, and fruit is gathered in. The custom of fireworks displays has been acquired from the Chinese traders.

During the Christmas holidays the natives are attired in their best suit—a singlet and new *lub-lub*, or it may be a short pair of white or khaki pants.

Although the natives in the vicinity of Rabaul at the present time lead a comparatively indolent life, there is reason to hope that as time goes on, they will become the owners of their own plantations, as most of the land still remains in the hands of the natives.

Wives are bought with so many yards of native money (small white shells threaded on a stick). If a boy steals another boy's Mary, he has to pay over as much as the first husband paid for her. This amicably settles the question, and all parties are satisfied. When a boy buys a Mary (becomes engaged), he puts up an ornamental sign made of grass, leaves, and cocoanut shells in front of his house. An illustration of this custom is given.

CHAPTER 12

Garrison Life at Rabaul

Rabaul is situated in Neu Pommern (New Britain), on the eastern shore of Simpsonshafen on a level stretch of ground lying at the foot of two mountains—extinct volcanoes—and a ridge of hills, on which is the small township of Namanula. Rabaul is laid out on the block principle, rows of trees being planted along each street, on either side and in the centre. All houses and buildings are of weatherboard, built well off the ground on piles; each house is surrounded by fine wide verandahs, which tend to make them cool on the hottest day. Hedges take the place of fences round most of the houses, while round many of them have been planted cocoanut palms and other ornamental trees of tropical climes.

The northern end of Rabaul has been set apart for Chinese and Japanese inhabitants, and it is here that both of these races can be seen following their native customs and habits. The Chinese portion of the population is quartered in large weatherboard buildings, and here are found *Waschmann* (laundries), tea and coffee rooms, stores where the natives trade, Chinese eating houses, butchers, tailors, bootmakers—also gambling dens and other ill-famed houses. The women work harder than many of the men, who occupy most of their time in the gambling dens, which are open almost continuously. China Town goes to bed at 4.30 a.m., notwithstanding the fact the bugle sounds "Lights Out" at 10 p.m. About a quarter to five—just before dawn—the butcher slaughters the pigs, and a few minutes later the Chinese are going about their day's business.

Boys of ten and twelve years of age are working away with needle and thread as if they were tailors of many years' experience. One youngster of about eight years escorts his mother through Rabaul selling the vegetables she carries. A trip through China Town gives the impression that the Chinese are quickly awaking from their long sleep, and not many years will pass before they will be reckoned among *the nations* of the world.

The residents of Jap. Town are mostly given to boat building and fishing. One Japanese boat-builder employs as many as two hundred hands at ordinary times.

East of Rabaul is a ridge of hills about 600 feet above sea level, and here are found the Government House, the hospital, the printing works, and several homes of the principal residents. The little settlement is known as Namanula. A couple of miles beyond these hills is the open sea, and at Namanula there is almost continuously a sea breeze which minimises danger from fever.

In the Government House grounds a wireless station was erected from parts brought from the station captured by the Australians at Bita Paka, and this placed the Expeditionary Force in direct communication with Port Moresby, whence a little press news was sometimes received—*sometimes*—for at one time it was over three weeks before any news came through, and whenever it did come, the information was usually so meagre that very little was known of what was going on in other parts of the world.

The natives in this portion of the island came into the town each morning from their villages with baskets of bananas, *pawpaws*, cocoanuts, pineapples, yams, shells, etc., trading them to the troops for tobacco, bully beef, biscuits, or anything that the natives desired to have and the men had no use for.

When the force landed at Rabaul, and guards had been placed round the town, buildings were set aside for various officers, stores, etc. The large three-storeyed store of the New Guinea Company was set aside as barracks for the right half battalion, "A," "B," "C" and "D" Companies, and 150 members of the R.A.N. R., the two upper floors being used as sleeping quarters

Changing guard at Rabaul.

for the men, while the ground floor was fitted up with tables and forms and used as a mess-room. The A.M.C., Transport and Signal Corps were quartered in suitable buildings. Residences in both Rabaul and Namanula were set aside for the use of officers and various details.

Timber, nails, and tools were in great demand by the men, who were soon busily engaged in making stretchers.

No time was lost in appointing men to civil positions in the Post Office, Treasury, Customs, and in forming a Fire Brigade. A bakery was erected so that the troops could have bread instead of biscuits, which required to be handled very carefully. To drop one on a comrade's foot was to evoke a flow of language more expressive than polite.

Bread was issued to the troops on Friday the 2nd October, for the first time since landing at Rabaul. Fresh meat was given out also the same day, but after a few days the familiar blue tins of bully beef were again in evidence, as the cold storage was unsatisfactory and all the meat went bad. It was not until the *Morinda* arrived at Rabaul on the 27th November, that fresh meat was again supplied to the garrison force, who greatly appreciated the change from bully beef and "fresh" herrings.

The food supply was a very serious question at one time. Expected stores had not arrived, and flour was bought at £22 per ton so that the men might have bread instead of biscuits. A search of all the stores in Rabaul and China Town revealed only thirty tins of jam. These went a long way amongst the eight hundred men! Some rice, sufficient for one ration, was obtained at an exorbitant price. The supply of sugar and tea had become exhausted. A little sugar could be obtained in China Town at 1/- per pound, while tea was half a crown a pound—and a poor class at that. The acuteness of the situation was relieved by the arrival of the *Meklong* from the Admiralty Islands with flour, tea, and sugar on board.

Most of the Germans were sent off to Sydney as prisoners. The few who were allowed to remain got themselves into disfavour with the garrison troops, and the following letter written by a member of the expedition neatly explains the circumstances:—

Botanical Gardens, Rabaul.   *No. 3. Skeleton of whale.*

We had a bit of excitement here last night. 'A' Company was marching past the house used by the Germans as a club when a couple of intoxicated Germans insulted the boys by shouting to them, 'Ha! Ve vill yet make you Engleesh tremble. Left, Right.' All the others showed their approval by loud guffaws and cheers. In our ranks something like thunder threatened, but the men, showing splendid behaviour and discipline under humiliating circumstances, continued on their march.

The hour of reckoning came and the debt was repaid with humorous interest. The lads held a mass meeting. The result of their deliberations was seen at about 7 p.m., when, headed by a cornet player, they marched off to the tune of 'It's a long way to Tipperary,' and arrived at the Club House, the musician playing the *Marsellaise*. After a ringing cheer the house was besieged, and Germans found under beds, in wardrobes, and outhouses were brought out struggling to the front verandah, where they were ordered 'Attention! Hats off!' We then sang 'God Save the King,' followed by three cheers for our good sovereign. We held an impromptu chorus concert, singing a number of the favourite songs, *viz.*, 'Rule Britannia; It's a long way to Tipperary; *Marsellaise*; Advance Australia Fair; This Bit of the World belongs to Us,' the latter with gusto. 'Sons of the Sea; For Auld Lang Syne; For He's a Jolly Good Fellow.'

Whilst we enjoyed the free use of our lungs, three men climbed on the roof, and in a short time the French tri-colour flag was fluttering in the breeze. Three more cheers were then given.

There was some trouble in getting a flag. A Union Jack was sought for but could not be found, so a handy man got three pieces of cloth, French colours, and sewed them together.

Just when the flag was hoisted an officer arrived with the guard to disperse us. The whole scene was executed with expedition and humour. The boys enjoyed it to the full.

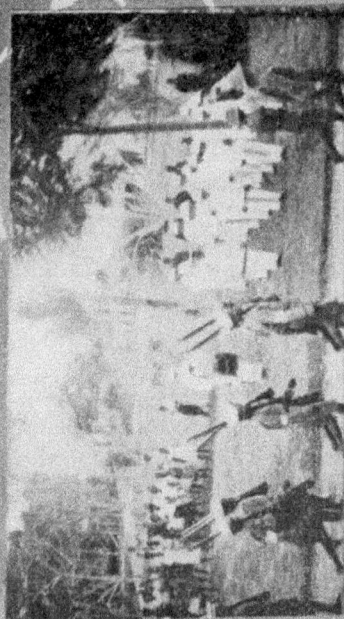

Hoisting of Flag at Rabaul, 13th September, 1914.

1. *Marching to Proclamation Square.*   2. *Native police boys.*   3. *Marching from ceremony.*

Some of the business wags had a good time drinking the Germans' beer while the latter were on parade. Responding to the command to return to quarters, we marched off to the tune of 'Rule Britannia,' and dispersed.

Most of the Germans were shareholders in the New Guinea Store, and next morning notices appeared in the barracks that any person found purchasing goods from the New Guinea Store would be publicly blanketed.

Soon after the episode related in this letter, the Casino was opened as a pastime club for the garrison troops. A billiard table, punching ball, set of gloves, quoits, etc., served to pass away many an evening. Provisions were made for the writing of letters, and one room was set aside as a reading room, where magazines, papers, and books could be read without fear of interruption.

To further relieve the monotony of garrison life, sports and concerts were arranged. Football and cricket matches were played between rival companies, and the garrisons at Rabaul and Herbertshohe. Between the naval and infantry members of the garrison there was keen competition in all branches of sport. In a shooting match, with German rifles and bullets, "C" Company won from "D" Company by a margin of three points.

Trafalgar Day was celebrated with a big sports meeting on Proclamation Square. January, 1915, was a busy month as far as sports and concerts were concerned. The profits from the dry and wet canteens had to be distributed amongst the men as prize money.

Notwithstanding the trying climate, the health of the garrison troops was on the whole good; the only case of death from sickness being that of AB. Gardner of the R.A.N. R., who contracted fever at Wilhelmshaven. He was buried at Rabaul beside the grave of Private Wates, who died as the result of a rifle wound, accidentally self-inflicted.

Holmes Avenue, Rabaul.

CHAPTER 13

Return Home to Sydney

After a few weeks, garrison life became very monotonous, and the continual question was "When are we going to leave here?" Although they had signed on for six months service, the majority of the men were anxious to return to Sydney so that they could re-enlist for active service in Europe.

The number of rumours (or buzzes as they were termed) about the return to Sydney and the number of vessels reported to be on their way to convey the troops home, was astonishing. If all the expected vessels had arrived, almost every vessel trading in Australian waters would have visited Australia's new territory.

Whenever a vessel was reported by any of the signal stations there was loud cheering amongst the troops, and much speculation as to whether the vessel was the *Berrima* come to take them back to Sydney. This occurred so frequently that before the troops did leave Rabaul an outburst of cheering on their part usually called forth the following remark from any natives that might be in the vicinity, "Urra, *Berrima* comin'."

Two cruisers, two destroyers and a store-ship flying the Japanese flag visited the harbour about Christmas time, and it was thought that they might convoy the troops back to Sydney, but the Japanese vessels only waited long enough to take in stores. In leaving the harbour the vessels of the fleet steamed round, and no doubt several particulars regarding the depth of the water, etc., have been noted for use at some future date maybe.

It was on the 17th December that the first sign of a relief

force was made. The *Eastern*, convoyed by the *Una*, entered Simpsonshaven at 11.30 a.m., and there was great pleasure amongst the men of the garrison when it was learned that the *Eastern* had 200 troops on board.

However, these troops were for the relief of men doing garrison duty at outlying islands, and only 250 men out of the 1,500 that had come away were sent home by the *Eastern* on the 9th January, and these men were mostly those who had been down with severe attacks of fever.

The administrator—Col. Holmes—and Col. Watson returned to Sydney in charge of these troops, and the command of the remainder devolved upon Col. Paton until their return to Sydney by the *Navua*, which arrived at Rabaul on the 9th February. The *Eastern* also returned from Sydney with a further 300 troops for garrison duty in the tropics, and on the 10th February all the troops of the First Australian Naval and Military Expedition still remaining in the islands embarked on the two vessels—200, including sick and invalided, on the *Eastern*, while 880 were embarked on the *Navua*.

The trip back to Sydney was marked by particularly calm weather, except for two days off the Queensland coast, where a hurricane was encountered. This delayed the vessels, but so anxious were the men to get home to "Sydney Town," that there were plenty of volunteer stokers available. Working willingly and continuously some of the lost time was soon made up.

On Thursday morning, 18th February, Sydney Heads were sighted, and the first of the welcome home was given by the crew of the pilot boat as the *Navua* passed into Port Jackson at 11.30 a.m.

Anchoring in Watson's Bay for a couple of hours the troops were examined by the medical officer, and, *pratique* being granted, the *Navua* moved into the E. & A. wharf at Circular Quay, where the *Eastern* was also berthed, having beaten the *Navua* by twenty-seven hours.

Steaming down the harbour the troops were welcomed back by the crowds on the ferry boats with cheer after cheer, while the vessels kept up an incessant blowing of whistles. This

Colonel Paton, V.D., in command of the troops on their return to Sydney.

brought crowds to the water front, and along Circular Quay was one mass of people.

The boat was not expected to arrive until Friday morning, when there was to be a march through the city to the barracks. To think of keeping over 800 men on the boat for eighteen hours, after they had been away for six months in a tropical land, and on unsuitable rations for the past two months, was unjust, to say the least. However, leave had already been granted the men when this order was received at the boat.

It was hard to believe that the smiling men who came off the *Navua* that afternoon were the same men who, only a few weeks before, had been scattered in the islands on garrison duty and living in tropical climates on bully beef and biscuits.

The march through the city on Friday morning was witnessed by many thousands of people. The naval reservists preceded the "boys in khaki" as far as Liverpool Street, where they formed a guard of honour for the infantry portion of the force, and then marched off to their depot at Rushcutter's Bay, while the troops went on to the Victoria Barracks, where equipment, rifles and bayonets were handed in and personal kit obtained.

The members of the force were discharged on Friday, 4th March, having completed the six months for which they had signed on. A large percentage are signing on again, but their desire is to go straight to the front and not to Egypt.

CHAPTER 14

G. R.—Proclamation

Proclamation on behalf of His Majesty George the Fifth, by the Grace of God, of the United Kingdom, and of the Dominions Overseas, King, Defender of the Faith, Emperor of India.

By Colonel William Holmes, D.S.O., V.D., Brigadier commanding His Majesty's Naval and Military Expeditionary Force.

Whereas the forces under my command have occupied the Islands of New Britain:

And Whereas upon such occupation the authority of the German Government has ceased to exist therein:

And Whereas it has become essential to provide for proper government of the said colony, and for the protection of the lives and property of the peaceful inhabitants thereof.

Now, I, William Holmes, Companion of the Distinguished Service Order, Colonel in His Majesty's Forces, Brigadier Commanding the aforesaid Expeditionary Force, do hereby declare and proclaim as follows:—

1. From and after the date of these presents, the island of New Britain and its dependencies are held by me in military occupation in the name of His Majesty the King.

2. War will be waged only against the armed forces of the German Empire and its Allies in the present war.

3. The lives and private property of peaceful inhabitants will be protected, and the laws and customs of the colony

will remain in force so far as is consistent with the Military situation.

4. If the needs of the troops demand it, private property may be requisitioned. Such property will be paid for at its fair value.

5. Certain officials of the late government may be retained, if they so desire, at their usual salaries.

6. In return for such protection, it is the duty of all inhabitants to behave in an absolutely peaceful manner, and to carry on their ordinary pursuits so far as is possible, to take no part directly or indirectly, in any hostilities, to abstain from communication with His Majesty's enemies, and to render obedience to such orders as may be promulgated.

7. All male inhabitants of European origin are required to take the oath of neutrality prescribed, at the garrison headquarters, and all firearms, ammunition and war material in the possession or control of inhabitants are to be surrendered forthwith, as is also all public property of the late government.

8. Non-compliance with the terms of the proclamation and disobedience of such orders as from time to time may be promulgated, will be dealt with according to Military Law.

9. It is hereby notified that this proclamation takes effect in the whole island of New Britain and its dependencies from this date. Given at Government House, Rabaul, this twelfth day of September, 1914.

William Holmes,
Brigadier Commanding.

Witness:

    Francis Heritage,
    Brigade-Major.

        God Save The King.

Proclamation

Read to Natives on the Annexation of the late German Possessions in the Pacific, Rabaul, September 12th, 1914.

All boys belonga one place, you savvy big master he come now, he new feller master, he strong feller too much, you look him all ship stop place; he small feller ship belonga him. Plenty more big feller he stop place belonga him; now he come here he take all place. He look out good you feller. Now he like you feller look out good alonga him. Suppose other feller master, he been speak you, "You no work alonga new feller master" he gammon. Suppose you work good alonga new feller master, he look out good alonga you, he lookout you get plenty good feller *kai-kai* (food); he no fightem black boy alonga nothing.

You look him new feller plag; you savvy him? He belonga British (English); he more better than other feller; suppose you been makem paper before this new feller master come, you finish time belonga him first; finish time belonga him, you like makem new feller paper longa man belonga new feller master, he look out good alonga you; he give good feller *kai-kai*.

Suppose you no look out good alonga him, he cross too much. English new feller master he like him black feller man too much. He like him all same you piccanin alonga him. You get black feller master belonga you, he all same police master. You look out place alonga him, he look out place alonga you. You no fight other feller black man other feller place, you no kai-kai man. You no steal Mary belonga other feller black man. Me finish talk alonga you soon. Bye-and-bye ship belonga new feller master he come; he look out place belonga you. You look out him now belonga place belonga you, you speak him all the same.

Me been talk alonga you now, now you give three good feller cheers belonga new feller master.

No More 'Um Kaiser.

God Save 'Um King.

Native Words

1. *Teeki*
2. *Owarooa*
3. *Owatool*
4. *Iwot*
5. *Ileema*
6. *Lepteeki*
7. *Lowarooa*
8. *Lowatool*
9. *Lowe wot*
10 *Awanoon*

Bamboo	*Akowrr*
Banana	*Mo or Ahwoondoo*
Cocoanut	*Coolow*
Paw–paw	*Me-me-ab*
Fowl	*Kokaroo*
Pig	*Aburra*
Water	*Ataba*
Salt Water	*Ata*
Come here	*Oonami*
Hurry up	*Ah-loo-loot*
Goodbye	*Yorkor*
Go away	*Oon-awunna*
You may go	*Dor-awunna*
Bring me	*Navee-lapeea*
Hill	*Bwana*
Chief	*Lului*
Finished	*Epahl*
Hair	*Grass*

Australia's First Naval & Military Expeditionary Force

MILITARY.

BRIGADE STAFF.

Holmes, Col. W.
Howse, Lieut.-Col. N. R.
Heritage, Major F. B.
Travers, Captain R. J. A.
Holmes, Lieut. B.
Wilkinson, S.S.M., W.
Brown, B.O.R.-Sgt. F. G.
Richards, B.O.R.-Cpl. C. J.

Privates.

Butler, L.
Driver, F.
Fortescue, F.
O'Hara, D.

HEADQUARTERS STAFF.

Watson, Lt.-Col. W. R.
Paton, Lieut.-Col. J.
Lane, Captain C. H. D.
Goodsell, Captain S. P.
Heritage, Lieut. K.
Sadler, Lieut. R. M.
Inglis, Warrant-officer W.
Garner, Quartermaster H.
Harris, Quartermaster E.
Hobbs, O.R.-Sgt. N. H.
Gray, Sgt.-drummer A. H.
Linklater, Pnr.-Sgt. R. L.
Williams, Sgt-cook A.
Baulch, Tspt.-Sgt. F. W.
Hanley, Sig.-Sgt. P. L.
Lane, Armr.-Sgt.

Siglr.-Privates.

Cooke, A. A.
Corrighan, W.
Ellis, H.
Facey, J. H.

Griffiths, G.
Morley, J. E.
Smith, G. H.
Walters, C.

Trst.-Privates.

Adams, G. H.
Arkinstall, J. H.
Bannister, F. S.
Blakeman, P. A.
Elliott, R. J.
Lavender, G.
Matthew, A.
Moorey, F. P.
Mortimer, P. W.
Prior, J. H.
Reid, C. B.
Rushbrooke, C. E. F.
Stewart, A. H.
Terrell, S. F.
Drummond, Orderly E. A.
Peadon, Orderly S. H.
Hudson, Batman B. L.
Lehmaier, Batman L. H.
Liddon, Batman G. W.
Moseley, Batman J. D'Arcy
M'Millan, Batman, J. M. ,
Pallister, Batman T.
Sandford, Batman F.
Webb, C. F.

Unattached.

Bruce, Captain H. L.
Chambers, Lieut. L. K.

MACHINE GUN SECTION.

Harcus, Capt. J. L.
Marsden, Lieut. T. R
Leslie, Sgt. W.

Stewart, Sgt. J.
Johnson, Corp. A. H.
Walsh, Corp. L. C.
Bate, Driver N. S.
Hall, Driver G. A. V.
Moynihan, Driver C. J.
Waygood, Driver F. B.

Privates.

Axtens, I. W.
Bates, A. R.
Burne, C.
Carmichael, J.
Clasper, J. G.
Cooke, E. G.
Eichler, A. M.
Eitel, C. C.
Ellis, A. G.
Evers, C. J.
Flack, A. K.
Glover, W. R.
Harris, R. R.
Hudson, A. B.
Jackson, E. E.
Kerslake, G.
Knapton, B. C.
Knowler, T.
Muller, W. B.
Nicholls, P. L.
Spearman, E. H.
Treloar, .E H.
Tennant, E.
Walklate, E. G.
Webb, R. C.
Withers, B. F.

"A" COMPANY.

Beardsmore, Major R. H.
Manning, Lieut. C. E.
Fry, 2nd Lt., W. A. Le R.
Mack, Col.-Sgt. G.
Anderson, Sgt. A. F.
Hardy, Sgt. A.
Lindsay, Sgt. T. J. E.
Sheppard, Sgt. W. H. S.
Blanchard, Cpl. N. G.
Hayes, Cpl. P.

Price, Cpl. B.
Smith, Cpl. W. E.

Privates.

Allard, G. G.
Andrews, H. A. J.
Barker, S. W.
Bennett, P.
Blake, I. M.
Blake, L. W.
Bolton, C. T.
Bond, F. E.
Braddon, A.
Brewster, F. E.
Brightwell, A. M.
Brown, H. G.
Brown, R. J.
Browne, R. M.
Browning, L. K. G.
Burghart, E. H.
Burke, M. F.
Chatting, G.
Clark, A. W.
Clark, B. P.
Cooper, F.
Cottam, F.
Davey, W. E.
Davie, W. C.
Deroubaix, J. A.
Desmond, W.
Devlin, E. G. N.
Donovan, F.
Dunn, C. E.
Dutton, S.
Edwards, G. M.
Eldershaw, A. G.
Ferris, S. R.
Field, —.
Fitzsimons, A. J.
Flemming, V.
Fox, J. R.
Fox, T. A.
Fraser, F. A. G.
Frendin, J. E.
Fuller, W. E.
Gallehawk, A.
Garden, N. H.
George, C

Gibb, J.
Goodenough, E. A.
Graham. W. J.
Gregory, C. F.
Guard, W. H. G.
Hance, C. E. A.
Hardy, C.
Hardy, C. A.
Hardy, W. H.
Hawkes, H. C.
Hay, R. J.
Heath, H.
Henley, H. L.
Henwood, N. J.
Hickey, G. S.
Hine, G. E.
Hodge, G. C.
Holman, T. E.
Howard. W. A.
James, J. G.
Jelfs, S. A.
Johnson, F. M.
Kane, H. E.
Kendrew, F. R.
Keyte, E. G.
Kilpatrick, W. S. C.
King, J. A.
Lane, J. B.
Lawson, J. C.
Lee. E. I.
Livingstone, T.
Mackenie, R.
Martin, S. S.
Mason, L. F.
Maulsbury, J. R.
Maundrell, J. D.
May, J. G
Moore, L. W.
McCrae, L. O.
McKay, G. C. C.
McLean, A. S.
Nelson, J. A. W.
Parker, B. A.
Pluck, R.
Plummer. G. E.
Pooley, W. G.
Pope, H. H.
Ridge, J.

Roy, B.
Satterley, J.
Shearston, H.
Stein, F. M.
Stewart, D.
Stone. R. G.
Streeton, F. H.
Upton, S. A.
Walker, J. A.
Walter, C. A.
Warr, G. S. A.
Watkin, S H.
Webb, T.
Wilson, T. J.
Wood, W.
Wright, J.

"B" COMPANY.

Norrie, Capt. E. C.
Fisher. Lieut. S. D.
Norman, Lieut. R. H.
Graham. Col.-Sgt. F. A.
Hill. Sgt. W.
Nowland, Sgt. R. C.
Robertson, Sgt. W. R. C.
Ferguson, Cpl. L. D.
Holdsworth, Cpl. J. A.
Moffatt, Cpl. J. S.
Manley, Cpl. A. E.
Milner, Cpl. J. S.
Dall, Pionr. R.

Privates.

Abbott, A.
Allen, R.
Armstrong, H.
Bannister, J. W.
Beeby, R.
Belwood, H. M.
Bendrodt, J. C.
Beston, P.
Bevill, R. R.
Blake, N. M.
Bone. W. J.
Boyd, J. F.
Broad,, D. G.
Burke, T. J.
Callaway, F. W. B.
Carmichael, J.

Champion, A. B.
Chisholm, W. N.
Clatworthy, T.
Clayton. C. E.
Clogg, A. J.
Collins, H.
Corey, P. B.
Dally, E. A.
Davenport, E. J.
Day, A. T.
Dickson, R.
Dodd, G.
Donohue, E. D.
Duncan, H. C.
Earl, A.
Edgington, A. H.
Fitzgerald, J. E.
Fogarty, J. M.
Garston, W. E.
Gay, W. H.
Gillard, W. G.
Golding, S. A.
Goodrich, E. P.
Gourlay, J. C. L.
Halyday, J.
Hely, C. E.
Henry, E.
Howard, H. C.
Janson, A. I.
Kemp, J. E.
Kendall, E. J.
King, W. E.
Kirkland, F. J.
Lakin, C.
Larken, G. W.
Lawton, M.
Lee, E.
Lumb, H.
Little. R. A.
Lovell, H.
Macfarlane, M. R.
Mascord, H. O.
Milne, H. S.
Mitchell, G.
Montefiore, C. G.
Montefiore, L. R.
Moore, G. W.
Morgan, W. B. S.

Morris, A.
Myers, F.
McGranger, H. H.
MacKenzie, W. G.
MacLaren, J.
MacRae, D. A.
Norman, E. R.
O'Brien, N.
Owen, A. P.
Paterson, R. B.
Pinks, A.
Pitt, S. J.
Porritt, W.
Porter, F. V.
Portman, V. B.
Rainey, A. E.
Reynolds, W. C.
Robinson, A. J.
Ross, R. M.
Roynham, M. L.
Rumsey, W. P.
Ryan, P.
Scott, E. I. C.
Scott-Holland, E. S.
Sheppard, O. J.
Snowdon, R. M.
Stewart, T. S.
Stone, G. A.
Stroud, W. H. R.
Swale, B. V.
Tate, H. V.
Telling, F.
Thomas, F. M.
Townshend, E.
Turton, A. A. G.
Waddell, W. R.
Wallace, E. W.
Walsh, W. H.
Wells, C. S.
Wiles, W. H.
Willing, W. R.
Whitehead, D. J. W.
Wood, J.
Yard, E. S.
Yarrington, W. R.

"C" COMPANY.
Grant-Thorold, Capt. R.

Partridge, Lieut. R.
Kirke, 2nd-Lieut. E. W.
Crook, Col.-Sgt. V. E.
Elliott, Sgt. D. S.
St. George, Sgt. T. R.
Hoskins, Sgt. A. K.
Crampton, Sgt. W. W.
Taylor, Cpl. C.
Leadbeater, Cpl. J.
Grace, Cpl. C. E.
Hart, Cpl. C. A. H.
White, Cpl. R.

Privates.

Arnold, R. E.
Bowden, A. R.
Bradford, J.
Broomfield, R. F. V.
Brigland, S. B.
Bryant, G. W.
Burrington, H. L.
Butterworth, G. G.
Carrick, P.
Collins, A. E.
Conray, P. J.
Conway, J. P.
Cookson, Signaller J. D.
Corrigan, L. J.
Courtney, G. R.
Coy, G.
Creed, R.
Croadsell, R. H.
Cullen, R. W.
Dawson, W. C. H.
Dean, J.
Delaney, H. A.
Delaney, P.
Donald, J.
Eather, J.
Fell, R.
Fitzgerald, C. R.
Flanagan, J.
Fox, R. E.
Fox, W. F.
Fripp, S. T.
Gregg, R. W.
Greig, D.
Graham, H. G.

Graham, N. C.
Gudgeon, J. E.
Gullofren, R. H.
Hall, P.
Harrald, C. J. B.
Hayes, O. N.
Healey, W. P.
Hocking, F. A. W.
Hodgson, B.
Holland, J. C. L.
Holman, A.
Howarth, D. T.
Hume, G.
Hunter, G. W.
Hunter, R. J.
Inman, H. H.
Irving, G.
James, A.
James, T. R.
James, W. B.
Jenkins, A. T.
Jones, F. A.
Jones, F. S.
Johnson, A. W.
Johnson, D.
Kearns, A. A.
Kearns, E. P.
King, Signl. H. J.
Lavender, G.
Laws, G. T.
Lear, J. H.
Lees, J. S.
Lenton, C. W.
Light, H. R.
Mason, E. B.
May, W. E.
Moore, A.
Mulford, E. A.
M'Donald, J. R.
M'Ginty, F. J.
M'Geechan, J.
M'Kenzie, R. B.
M'Pherson, J. E.
Nowland, A. M.
O'Connor, J. L.
O'Donnell, R. J. C.
O'Keefe, D. P.
Philpot, G. H.

Pratt, E. K.
Reyner, J. R
Scanlon, W. H.
Schiedel, N. P.
Shepherd, J.
Skinner, W. J.
Smith, C. S.
Solomon, M.
Stanley, J. M.
Stillman, K. P.
Sullivan, D. P.
Sullivan, K. P.
Szablowski, J.
Taylor, C. S.
Taylor, C. H.
Telford, J.
Thorpe, E. A.
Thring, F. G.
Tomlinson, T.
Toohey, W.
Walker, S. W.
Wallace, F. D.
Wallach, R.
Ward, H. B.
Wates, A. M.
Welch, A.
Wells, H. J.
Whitehead, E.
Whitehead, F.
Wilkin, W. M.
Williams, W.
Williamson, R. C.

"D" COMPANY.

MacPherson, Capt. T. R.
Ravenscroft, Lieut. L. B.
McDowell, 2nd Lieut. J. A.
Burns, Col.-Sgt. M. B.
Penly, Sgt. W. C. M.
Oliver, Sgt. G. W.
Smith, Sgt. A. W. A.
Casey, Sgt. J. J.
White, Cpl. A. C.
Acheson, Cpl. W.
Graham, Cpl. W. C.
Wilson, Cpl. J. R.
Gitshan, Cpl. T. L.
Milne, Cpl. F. R.

Brydie, Cpl. A.
French, L.-Cpl. J. A.
Maunder, L.-Cpl. H.
Harber, Signaller O. L.
Hardman, Bugler, J. P.
Sproule, Bugler J. W.
Dawson, Driver W. E. V.
Martin, Driver T. J.
Clarke, Pioneer C. E.

Privates.

Baker, E. W.
Bayley, K.
Besson, W.
Bingham, J. F.
Bovard, J. A.
Breeze, E. G. G.
Bullock, G. R.
Burger, A.
Cameron, L.-Cpl. J.
Carr, W. J.
Challenor, G. T.
Churchill, W. J.
Clarke, W. E.
Coker, C. W.
Coles, S. H.
Crothers, D. T.
Cunningham, E. A.
Darby, A. K.
Davey, H.
Dean, R. A.
Deny, H. M.
Dessaix, R. S. D.
Diehl, J.
Dixon, J. A.
Dixon, L.
Dixon, T.
Dowling, W. H.
Doyle, L.-Cpl. F. J. M.
Driscoll, C. A.
Eather, T. R. L.
Ebbrell, C. I.
Edwards, E. J.
Farley, W. M.
Fenton, W. W.
Finlayson, G. J.
Fleming, F.
Fraser, W. A.

Friedman, H. E.
Gallafent, A. E.
Garland, H. F. E.
George, S. A.
Gray, T. J.
Grayham, T. L.
Groves, L.
Groves, J. A.
Hampton, D. R.
Harrison, L. J.
Hawke, S.
Healey, M. D.
Heeps, J. V.
Higgins, K. A.
Hollebon, L.-Cpl. E.
Homden, L. G.
Honeyman, V.
Hoskins, A. H.
Hoyle, G. E.
Hunter, R.
Hyde, J. J.
Johnson, E.
Johnston, H. K.
Jowers, F.
Jowers, W. H.
Kelly, A. E.
Knight, S. B.
Lawson, R. V. A.
Lovett, A. H.
Leer, S. C.
Lowry, W. J.
Merritt, E. W.
Morrison, J. W.
Morrison, W. M.
M'Glashan, F.
M'Kinnon, W. J.
Oldfield, E. J.
Pery, V. H.
Price, W.
Punch, P. O.
Ramsay, R.
Rea, H.
Reeves, Signl. L. C.
Roberts, C. R.
Roberts, R.
Saunders, F.
Smedley, H. W.
Tanner, H. R.

Thomson, S. W.
Vince, C. H.
Watkins, W. R.
Weidner, V. J. M.
Welch, E. V.
White, L.-Cpl. M. J.
Whiteford, H. E.
Whiteside, R.
Woods, F. J.

"E" COMPANY.

Morrison, Capt. H. L.
McLachlan, Lieut. B. H.
Manning, 2nd Lieut. G.
Buchanan, Col.-Sgt. F.
Tibby, Sgt. F. A.
Wright, Sgt. J. K.
Gordon, Sgt. W. J.
Carlyle, Sgt. F.
Macqueen, Cpl. L. S.
Macqueen, Cpl. W. H.
Black, Cpl. W. I.
Otter, Cpl. H. W.
Curnow, Cpl. H. W.
Wilmott, L-Cpl. J. L.
Godwin, L.-Cpl. S. B.
Lee, L.-Cpl. A. E.

Privates.

Abbott, H. W.
Adams, L. W.
Adams, T.
Anderson, A. G.
Anderson, A. M.
Bale, W. G.
Bawn, S.
Beatson, W.
Berry, A. J.
Blackburn, G. H. B.
Boyd, A. H.
Brown, W. C.
Bullock, E.
Bush, B. O.
Bush, E. C.
Buttle, W. E.
Casey, J. J.
Chisholm, A.
Clark, F. S. M.

109

Clark, F. W.
Clarke, J. B.
Clemence, J. E.
Collins, E. L.
Coombes, H. L.
Cornell, W. G.
Cox, A.
Cox, G. F.
Crisp, S S.
Dare, C. R.
Doody, J. J.
Downes, A.
Drummond, A.
Drysdale, G. H.
Dundas, E. L.
Dunn, C. S.
Falle, L. P.
Ferguson, J.
Fisk, A.
Frazer, E. F.
Fry, J.
Gallagher, C.
Grace, E.
Griffiths, G. N.
Green, T. W.
Guy, T. L.
Hall, H. P. N.
Harber, C. S.
Harris, H. G.
Harrison, R. S.
Harvey, T.
Hodge, L.
Holland, C. S.
Holm, A. L.
Howard, T. W.
Hunter, R.
Jackson, J. C.
James, A.
Jenkins, T. O.
Jones, J. J.
Letton, K. S.
Lark, P. F.
Larsen, C. P.
Lee, R. M.
Lee, G.
Martin, S. F.
Mehan, D. N.
Mitchell, T.

Moores, R.
M'Carthy, J.
Neave, G.
Nelson, H.
Pallisser, T.
Paton, D. M.
Pickett, C. H. J.
Plane, A. A.
Plane, L. G.
Pope, A. R.
Poulton, G.
Presgrave, S. A.
Rivers, C. W.
Robertson, N. R.
Robertson, T. B.
Rodini, F. J.
Shaw, E. R.
Sheppard, F.
Smith, J. D.
Smith, L. A.
Smith, V.
Smith, W. J.
Snodgrass, R. E.
Sparkes, S. H.
Stephenson, G.
Sulivan, P. A.
Taylor, R. J.
Teale, A. J.
Thomason, W. A.
Tilbrook, W. C.
Turner, L. G.
Turner, S. G.
Vere, E. H.
Victorsen, E. M.
Walters, R.
Wasson, S. R.
Watts, H.
Watson, A. F.
Webb, F.
Wyatt, J. W.
Williams, G. J.
Willmott, S. L.
Wilson, W.

"F" COMPANY.

Twynam, Capt. E.
Maughan, Lieut. J. E.

Cooper, 2nd Lieut. A. L.
Luffman, Col.-Sgt. B.
Keleghan, Sgt. W.
Kimpton, Sgt. J. E.
Plimer, Sgt. J.
Schofield, Sgt. L. N.
Caller, Cpl. F. C.
Carpenter, Cpl. U. W.
Mair, Cpl. W. S.
Sayell, Cpl. A. J.
Tregear, Cpl. A. R.
Whitfield, Cpl. N. H.

Privates.

Aldham, J. H.
Allen, F. H.
Arthur, H. J.
Ashton, G. R.
Atkins, H.
Ayres, A. R.
Ballerum, F. C. W.
Beaman, T. E.
Bennett, L.
Bentley, C. B.
Berry, P.
Blackett, B. J.
Briant, H.
Brooks, B. G.
Buchanan, A. M. C.
Buchanan, F. W.
Burke, E.
Carthew, J.
Chapman, F. J.
Clancy, L. A.
Connelly, E. A.
Cranston, D. S.
Davies, J. N. C.
Davis, T. G.
Day, F. H.
Dennis, D. M.
Douglas, P. A.
Doyle, R.
Dunham, W. F.
Dunn, G. G.
Ewart, C. B.
Ferguson, W. I.
Fish, T.
Fleming, W. H.

Flethcher, J.
Forth, Signaller G. F O.
Fotheringham, L. G.
Hardwick, R.
Harper, H. D.
Hughes, D. R. A.
Jones, S. H.
Jones, T. H.
Keys, W. P.
Lagerlow, H. W.
Langworhty, A.
Laycock, J.
Lewins, N. T.
Mainstone, A.
Martin, J. W.
Maskell, A.
Mahony, B.
Merrett, C. E.
Merrett, F. E. S.
Myers, F.
Middlemiss, F.
Miles, Signaller R. F.
Mitchell, J. R.
Morris, R. A.
Morris, R. B.
Myers, H.
M'Donald, E.
M'Kay, A. J. W.
Neate, T. W. L.
Newton, H. E.
Nowell, J.
Oag, J. A.
Palmer, C. L.
Parkin, W.
Pearce, H. G.
Pittard, W. H.
Plumb, P.
Preece, W. E.
Prescott, J.
Rankin. W. E.
Reid, J.
Reid, J. H.
Reid, J.
Reynolds, R. L.
Roberts, H.
Ronald, H.
Ross, R. D.
Ross, W.

Russell, N. C.
Rutter, —.
Seale, J.
Shelley, G. V.
Small, G.
Smith, J.
Smith, J. W.
Smith, N. F.
Solomon, S.
Stevenson, A.
Sullivan, S.
Tait, W. G.
Tattersall, J.
Taylor, E. A.
Teale, W.
Therwell, C.
Thomlinson, R. B.
Thompson, K. H.
Walker, J.
Walters, W. G.
Webb, H W.
Wemyss, J.
Westbury, F| H.
Williams, A. H.
Williamson, S. W|
Williamson, W.
Wyborn, E. R.
Young, J. J.

"G" COMPANY.

Ralston, Major
Westgarth, Lieut.
Bruce, Lieut.
Henry, Col.-Sgt. J. D'A.
Anderson, Sgt.
Simpson, Sgt.
Linklater, Sgt.
Curtis, Sgt. P. H.
Davidson, Sgt.
Nunn, Sgt.
Souter, Cpl. J. J.
Robertson, Cpl. R.
Glover, Cpl. W. H.
Wallace, Cpl. A. A.
Verney, Cpl. R.
Watson, L.-Cpl. T. W.
Lyons, L.-Cpl. W. M.
Beesley, L.-Cpl. E. G.

Seymour, L.-Cpl. R. L.
Lyons, L.Cpl. L.
Jones, Pioneer A. L.
Davis, Pioneer A.
Hitchcock, Signaller R. G.
Wilson, Signaller W. E.
Jones, Signaller F. A.
Richards, A. E.
Johnson, F. M.
Lawler, P.
Underwood, A.
O'Hare, A.
Turner, H. G.
Phillip, T.

Privates.

Avard, L.
Ainsworth, V H. C.
Anderson, A. J.
Anderson, P. C.
Anderson, M.
Ashmen, P. C.
Ballington, P. G.
Blumenthal, S. J.
Bone, W. S.
Bower, A. W.
Campbell, R. B.
Charlton, A. H.
Clune, G.
Connolly, E. H.
Cooper, K.
Cross, L. H.
Croydon, P. M.
Currington, F.
Dunham, C. W.
East, F. L.
Eyles, W. C.
Evans, E. C.
Flood, J. P.
Hall, H. J.
Horgan, T. S.
Johnson, C. A.
Jullien, W.
Kirkness J. D.
Levy, C. J.
Linsley, G.
Louche, H. J.
Luff, H.

Menfing, J.
McFadden, E. A.
McGovern, J.
McGrath, W.
Nagle, W. J.
Neale, A. E.
Nelson, C. P.
Nelson, H. D.
New, S.
Newman, F. A.
Newman, F.
Nicholson, O.
Niven, C. A.
Noble, S.
Norton, A. R .
Oakes, A. N.
O'Brien, W. B.
Ogilvie, J. M.
O'Halloran, L. J. C.
Parsons, R. E.
Plummer, J.
Poynting, J. F.
Redmond, J. P. (Tony)
Richards, W. .
Roberts, C. .
Roberts, E. W.
Ross, C. A.
Ryan, A. E.
Smith, E. S.
Smith, R. A. W.
Smith, W. D.
Stuckey, C. R.
Tanzer, H. A.
Thomson, H.
Thorpe, J. L.
Torpy, J. B.
Turner, E. J.
Tucker, S. E.
Vanderberg, A. F.
Venn, A.
Vincent, W. C.
Walls, S.
Ward, E. J.
Watriama, W. J.
Wilkie, W. J.
Wolf, A. V.
Woolley, G. S.
Young, J.

" H " COMPANY.

Martin, Major E. F.
Sampson, Lieut. V. H. B.
Sherbon, 2nd Lieut. I. B.
Langtry, Col.-Sgt. H.
Crombie, Sgt. W. A.
Hunt, Sgt. F. W.
Milne, Sgt. H. S.
Barnes, Cpl. A. B.
Thomas, Cpl. G.
Reid, Cpl. E. H.
Monro, Cpl. E. E.
Carnell, 2nd Cpl. J. W.
Cole, 2nd Cpl. F. H.
Porter, 2nd Cpl. G. M.
Jenkins, 2nd Cpl. G. B.

Privates.

Adams, A. L. K.
Baker, S.
Banks, J. H.
Barrington, W. G. A.
Bartlett, J. R. H.
Baylis, S. T.
Beckton, S. J.
Bell, J. C.
Booth, H. R.
Bousfield, T.
Boyd, E. D.
Bradhurst, H.
Bragg, R. L.
Briggs, A. D.
Brodigan, E. B.
Brown, F. G.
Bruce, J. E. A.
Buckland. J. F.
Butler, J. L.
Cawley, T. W.
Clancy, J. S.
Collins, R. P.
Clempson, J.
Cooker, G. W.
Dahl, E. P.
Dallas, G.
Davis, J. P.
Demestre, E.
Denovan, H. G.

Evans, C. C.
Ferns, C.
Ford, H.
Frahm, W. A.
Garnon, D. H.
Gobert, C. A.
Griffin, G. St. C.
Grose, H.
Guthrie, A. C.
Hall, A. T.
Hammond, W. J.
Harris, R.
Hayes, H. H.
Hillier, F.
Hunt, A.
Hynes, W. J.
Jones, P. D.
Kempton, E. V.
King, W. J.
Kristensen, H. K.
Kyriako, A.
Lang, W. J.
Lawson, J. C.
Lee, B.
Leyne, J. I.
Lynch, D. H.
Lynch, P.
Lyons, J. M.
Macdonald, A.
Macfarlane, S. J.
Marshall, A.
Maughan, P. K.
Meek, J. G.
Meek, L. W.
Moffatt, W. R.
Montroy, H. P.
Moore, F. J.
Murray, J. D.
McCredden, R. D.
McGill, F. McC.
Newing, H. J.
Northcott, A. N.
O'Hara, D.
O'Brien, E. A.
Paidas, N.
Paulin, J.
Peterson, C. W.
Poole, F. T.

Powell, G. W. B.
Randall, H. W.
Ratsey, S. G.
Reid, R. J.
Renshaw, F. W.
Reynolds, H
Rice, H.
Richards, G. J.
Richmond, A. H.
Rigley, A. W.
Rogers, H. L.
Rose, W.
Rowlinson, S.
Ryan, E.
Saunders, T. L.
Sendall, H. L.
Shaw, H. E.
Sketheway, T. W.
Smart, S. W.
Smith, E. P.
Steer, R. L.
Stewart, S. P.
Stone, A. J.
Sullivan, R. V.
Summerscales, P.
Taylor, F. W.
Tonkin, J. E.
Trafford, H.
Trenouth, G.
Wakley, M.
Waldon, A. O.
Watson, J. W.
Watson, W. T.
Watt, J. C.
Weir, A. H.
Williams, W. A.
Wilson, F. J.
Woolley, G. S.
Young, E. L. C.

ARMY MEDICAL CORPS.

Maguire, Capt. F. A.
Donaldson, Capt. G. E.
Pockley, Capt. B. C. A.
Hazlitt, W.O. H.
Ward, Staff-Sgt. J. H.

Wray, Staff-Sgt. Dispenser
    R. M. F.
Mobbs, Sgt.-Clerk L. J.
Spears. Sgt. E. D.
Ellis, Cpl. J. A.
McCulloch, Cpl.-Cook
    J. W. H.

Privates.

Ahearn, H. A. J.
Bird, R. J.
Craig, J. E.
Daly, C. N.
Davies, T. A.
Dodson, W. L.
Drummond, C.
Forster, J. L. B.
Gale, N. S. W.
Gates, A. T.

Gooch, N. R.
Goodman, D. W.
Harvey, G. V.
Henderson, J. K.
Jifkins, C. E.
King, C.
Lonsdale, H. E.
McBride, G.
Owen, L. C.
Poole H. R.
Richardson, W.C. C.
Riches, W. A.
Robinson, F. H.
Smith, C. W.
Stanley, F. B.
Tovey, W.
Turnbull, W. J.
Walters, J. H.
Withers, H. C.

NAVAL.

BRIGADE STAFF.

Stevenson, Capt.
Livesay, Paymaster
Blackmore Petty Officer
Gosling, Officers' Steward

NAVAL STAFF.

Beresford, Commander
Bracegirdle, Lieut.-Com.
Hunter, Singnal Bos'n
William, Midshipman
McDonough, C.P.O.
Dyer, P.O.

BATTALION STAFF.

Browne, Lieut.-Com.
Elwell, Lieut.-Com.

No. 1 COMPANY.

Lambton, Commander
Hicks, Midshipman C. W.
Algie, W. G. L.

Banbury, G. H.
Bertram, W. J.
Bingham, L.
Bird, R.
Brown, F.
Buckland, W. G.
Callow, A.
Campbell, J. N.
Canham, C.
Carmarsh, H.
Cashin, R. H.
Catton, T.
Cave, A. S.
Clarke, G.
Clements, L.
Connell, A. C.
Connor, H.
Cummins, W. T.
Dalzell, A. G.
Dunningham. J. C.
Durston, W.
Eccleston, A. W.
Eccleston, J.
Evennett, N. S.

Eves, J.
Fuller, —.
Grice, E.
Harris, W. H.
Harslett, C.
Hidden, R. F.
Hood, A.
Jones, A. E.
Kenny, C. W.
Kerr, W.
Knight, P.
Lang, A. W. H.
Lawton, C.
MacKinnon, D.
Mallit, T.
Manning, N.
McFarlane, J. E.
Morehouse, S.
Nugent, B.
Ogilvie, J.
O'Sullivan, —.
Pointer, L.
Power, S M.
Richards, H. B.
Rigley, —.
Robertson, J.
Robertson, E. W.
Samuels, W. A.
Sharpe, H.
Smith, C. C.
Smith, W. S.
Stapleford, R.
Stephen, C.
Taylor, A.
Tange, A. J.
Thomas, L. C.
Thorpe, H. K.
Turner, W. R.
Watson, J. F. V.
Watson, J.
Williams, R. W.
Wood, S. C.
Hawkes, J.
Dewsbery, H.
Ashton, G. F.

No. 2 COMPANY.

Bowen, Lieut.-Com.

Read, Lieut.
Sage, Midshipman
Petersen, Gunner
Harris, P.O. G. M.
Briggs. P.O.
Fisk, P. O.
Barnes, P.O.
Kingsford, P.O.
Hamilton, P.O.
Adam, —.
Brown, H. A.
Bennett, E. H.
Berry, W.
Conlon, J.
Connor, H. O.
Cahill, G.
Cargill, H.
Chambers, A.
Dunn, J.
Davies, J.
Doodson, C. E.
Elliott, W.
Firth, G.
Fuz, E.
Fox, J.
Gardner, H.
Gresley, P.
Gunn, T. W.
Johns, J.
Johnson, F.
Jurd, F. G
King, R.
Lardner, J.
Light, T.
Miller, J.
Mitchell, —.
McKinnon, R.
McFarlane, H.
Parmenter, E.
Purcell, J.
Robins, H. H.
Rogers, H.
Smith, —.
Strike, S. W.
Stevens, J.
Sayers, G.
Southerley, A.
Stirton, J. L.
Stuart, D. C.

116

Sykes, F.
Thompson, J.
Wanless, N. A.
Williams, R. W.
Wright, F.

No. 3 COMPANY.

Gillan, Lieut
Sage, Midshipman
Ashton, H. A.
Adam, J.
Beaton, N.
Burnes, J.
Bruce, L. W.
Barry Thos.
Bundy, W. F.
Challinor, W. E.
Carrick, J. B.
Coombes, W. E.
Duffy, A.
Dunn, E.
Doyle, J. N.
Eccleston, J.
Eves, A. T.
Eskrigge, J. E.
Frawley, M.
Gunner, J. A.
Giddey, J. C
Grey, S. E. W.
Green, J.
Gemton, O. C.
Huntsman, F.
Humphries, S. J.
Harris, A. E.
Howton, W.
Howes, E. S.
John, E. F.
Jones, S.
Jamieson, W.
Knight, F.
Loneghan, P.
Lane, W. J.
Loughlan, S. F.
Learoid, N.
Lawson, J.
McIntyre, R. S.
McClure, R. S.
McKinnon, D.

Mackie, B.
McMahon, M. J.
Mannell, E.
Mosley, A. G.
Mollison, J.
Maddock, W. J.
Murray, W R.
McCourt, H.
Nicholls, J.
Nicholls, J.
Poole, D.
Peach, S. A.
Pearce, J.
Pelquest, E.
Rees, W.
Smith, V. W.
Smith, T. H.
Stuart, D. C.
Spencer, H. J.
Stanhope, L. J.
Seberg, L. B.
Sherry, J.
Stacey, W. W.
Spain, R. J. S.
Tindall, D. S.
Trembett, A. W.
Whitcher, E. A.
Wright, F
Whieley, C.
Wilson, T.
Watkins, G.

No. 4 COMPANY

Webber, Lieut.
Buller, Midshipman
Allen, W.
Annear, W.
Bensley, C.
Boyd, R.
Bennett, W.
Beglen, P.
Butler, E.
Bowme, E.
Benty, J.
Currie, F
Curwin, R.
Cook, C.
Cardoe, T.

Campbell, H.
Congues, A.
Dunslow, S. E.
Dumbleton, J.
Everest, W.
Eastman, L.
Elliott, —.
Fraser, J.
Fowler, R.
Gaulton, F.
Hooks, T.
Hunt, G.
Hughes, T. J.
Hammerberg, R.
Harris, C.
Harris, C.
Harrison, P. R.
Heggie, W.
Hale, F.
Hall C. F.
Jarrett, S. G.
Jeffries, B.
Janes, L.
Knox, W.
Looby, W. J.
Lawrence, C.
Lock, W.
Miles, L.
McDonald, G. R.
Miles, E.
McCarron, T.
McLachlan, D.
McLachlan, W.
Mitchell, A.
Martin, R. L.
Munford, H.
McDonald, N.
Palmer, G. R.
McDonald, N.
Palmer, G. R.
Pithouse, N.
Parfrey, H. H.
Orpen, H. R.
Osborne, F.
Robinson, A. W.
Ridley, E. R.
Ross, D.
Richardson, W.

Redfern, W. G.
Staines, S.
Stubbs, J.
Smith, T.
Smith, M. M.
Spunner, G.
Trickey, S.
Taylor, F.
Turner, W. R.
Tonkin, W. T.
Taylor, W.
Urquart, C.
Watford, J.
Willans, V.
Wickham, R.

No. 5 COMPANY.

Hext, Lieut.
Cock, Midshipman
Anderson, A.
Allison, A.
Alford, C. R.
Ballard, C. B.
Ball, G. S.
Brown, H. A.
Bartlett, J. W.
Beton, J. H.
Burgess, C. B.
Cluterbuck, E.
Clarke, A.
Capner, F. C.
Collier, P.
Day, L. A.
Dwyer, W. B.
Doyle, E.
Eadie, H.
Erickson, D.
Elkins, W.
Guller, J.
Graham, C.
Gillespie, J. A.
Gothard, W. M.
Guthrie, G. A.
Goldie, R. W.
Hemming, W.
Hoffmann, C. F.
Hattrick, R.

Henderson, S.
Hamilton, G.
Hartwell W.
Hudson, W.
Holmes, A. H.
Jones, J.
Johnstone, P.
Keiller, C.
Lang, J.
McIlwraith, J. T.
McVinsh, G.
Mitchell, W.
Merrick, H. J.
McLaren, O. G
Noble, R. J.
Nicholls, C.
Philp, J. C.
Parkin, C.
Parlett, W. C.
Patterson, W. C.
Phillpott, C.
Robertson, F.
Roberts G. G.
Scott, W.
Sercombe, W. G.
Simpson, M. E.
Sundstorm, G.
Sinel, J. F.
Smith, E. W.
Thomas, W.
Thompson, J.
Thorsby, C. V.
Woodrow, F. G.
Woolard, A. E
Warburton, W. F.
Wilson, J. H.
White, F. F.
Waltisbuhh, J.
Wiltshire, H. W.
White, J.
Webber, J.

No. 6 COMPANY.

Bond, Lieut.
Veale, Midshipman.
Allen, W.
Byrne, P.

Barnes, J. C.
Beatty, J.
Cameron, W.
Cookley, J.
Crow, G.
Coull, J.
Clarke, W.
Connolly, W.
Dugan, J.
Devescive, M.
Day, W.
Dodson, J.
Edminston, J.
Evans, J. O.
Edwards, A. D.
Fox, T. P.
Foreman, J.
Gwynne, J.
Godhon, H. C.
Grant, R.
Greaves, H. L. N.
Harvey, J.
Instance, F.
Ide, H.
Johnson, A.
Jackson, R.
Kuhn, C.
Leslie, D.
Loan, J.
Lockyer, H. C.
Lambert, H.
Lay, R.
Mullins, S. D.
Murch, J.
Mills, A.
Marshall, P.
McGuire, A.
Nelson, H.
Nelson, J. P.
Plate, H.
Perryman, C. P.
Parker, H.
Palmer, F. W.
Reaby, E. H.
Read, C.
Rogers, G.
Ricketts, J. E.
Renton, R.

Rutzon, A. A.
Rostrom, J.
Ricketts, C. J
Sangster, J. B.
Stewart. W.
Sawford. D.
Slack, H.
Santry, E.
Stuart, R.
Sinclair, G.
Steinthal, A. B.

Sangster, W.
Sawford, E. A.
Sawford, V. W.
Slee, A. C. R.
Simmons, Ed.
Taylor, F. G.
Vidiato, A.
Watson, H.
Worthington, A.
Wainwright, L.
Williams, H. C.

MEMBERS OF NAVAL GUNS CREW WHO LANDED AT HERBERTSHOHE, SEPT. 11, 1914.

Chief P.O, Gun. M. H. B.
    Richards, R.A.N., in
    charge
P.O. J. P. Sweeney, R.A.N.
    (H.M.A.S. *Sydney*)
A.S. W. Ward, R.A.N.
    (H.M.A.S. *Sydney*)
A.S. W. B. Neill, R.A.N.
    (H.M.A.S. *Sydney*)
A.S. J. A. Harte, R.A.N.
    (H.M.A.S. *Sydney*)
R. Hidden, R.A.N.R.
T. Catton, R.A.N.R.

D. Gunn, R.A.N.R.
G. H. Bambury, R.A.N.R.
L. Bingham, R.A.N.R.
H. Connor, R.A.N.R.
W. J. Bertram, R.A.N.R.
N. Manning, R.A.N.R.
A. G. Dalzell, R.A.N.R.
A. E. Jones, R.A.N.R.
R. W. Williams, R.A.N.R.
H. Sykes, R.A.N.R.
W. S. Smith, R.A.N.R.
T. Light, RA.N.R.

Australasia Triumphant
By A. St. John Adcock

Patrolling the Pacific

Whilst the new armies were still training, the fleet of Australia put to sea, joined the New Zealand fleet, and together they
proceeded to co-operate with the British naval forces in sweeping the Pacific for German merchantmen, and hunting down
the few elusive German cruisers that were prowling the seas
thereabouts in search of prey. Three of these cruisers in particular, the *Gneisenau*, the *Scharnhorst*, and the *Emden*, were dodging
all pursuit, successfully capturing and sinking British and French
trading and passenger ships, and bombarding the coast towns of
some of our South Sea Islands; and the *Emden*, before it could
be rounded up and destroyed, had gone as far afield as India and
shelled Madras. An Australian naval officer wrote home:

> The German cruisers are playing a game of hide-and-seek
> on the broad expanse of the Pacific, and are avoiding a
> trial of strength with the vessels of the Australian fleet. We
> have been looking for them ever since war was declared,
> and are more than anxious to have a go at them, but they
> keep out of the way. The task of definitely locating them
> and getting to grips is an enormous one. The Pacific is so
> wide, and there are so many thousands of islets that we
> could pass within five minutes of them and yet fail to be
> aware of their presence.
>
> Once they are cornered, it will be a fine fight—a fight to
> a finish. . . . Once we thought we had the German boats

bottled up in Simpson Haven. Orders were issued to the destroyers to ferret them out, and in the dead of night the three little boats, with all lights out and crews at their stations, crept into the harbour, which might have been mined. However, after sweeping round the bay we found our quarry was not there. We landed a small party which smashed up the telegraphic instruments, then dashed out again.

So, for some weeks the warships of Australia and New Zealand were alertly at work, chasing the nimble Germans in and out among those thousand islands of the South Seas. British and French and Japanese vessels took up the difficult hunt with them, but in that vast wilderness of waters, with such innumerable creeks and bays and obscure hiding-places to skulk in, it was far easier to lose the wily enemy than to find him. In due course, however, the *Gneisenau* and the *Scharnhorst* were cornered and accounted for; but the *Emden* remained at large and ran a long and brilliantly triumphant career before it was trapped and beaten at last in a desperate fight with the Australian battle cruiser, the *Sydney*.

Meanwhile, on the 30th August, 1914, the island of Samoa was captured without opposition by the combined fleets of Australasia, Britain, and France, under the command of Rear-Admiral Patey. When the fleets arrived off the island, the admiral sent an officer ashore with a letter to the acting governor, Herr S. N. Rimburg, saying:

I have the honour to inform you that I am off the port of Apia with an overwhelming force, and in order to avoid unnecessary bloodshed, I will not open fire if you surrender immediately. I therefore summon you to surrender to me forthwith the town of Apia and the Imperial possessions under your control. An answer must be delivered within half an hour to the bearer.

To some of us now there seems a touch of unconscious humour in Herr Rimburg's reply, when we remember how the ships of his own nation bombarded unfortified English towns

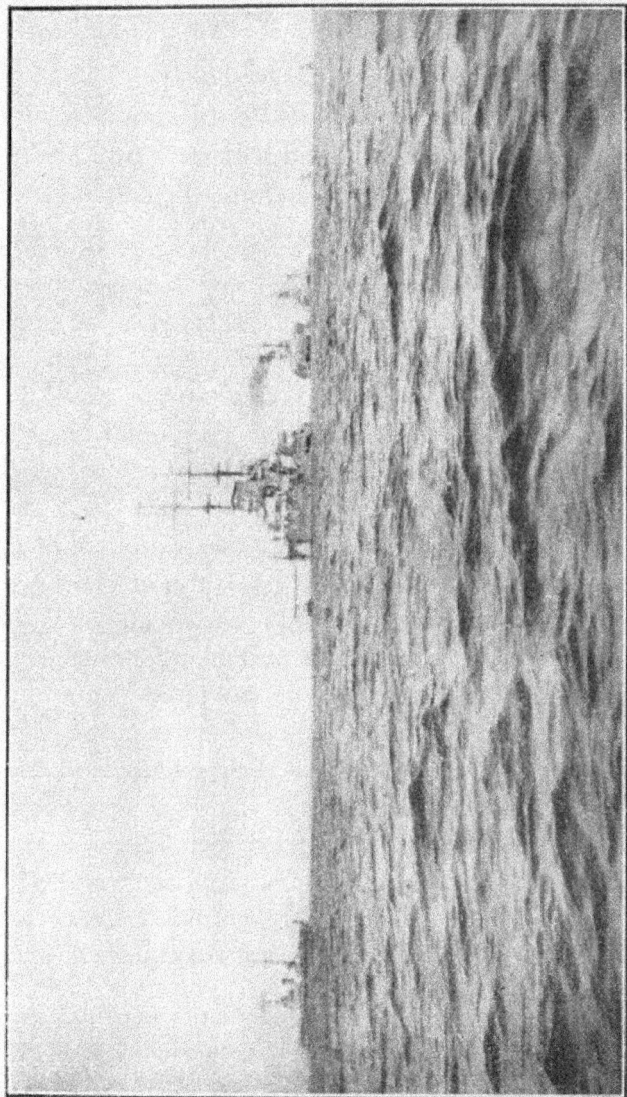

German Pacific Fleet (since sunk off Falkland Islands by Vice-Admiral Sturdee's Fleet) entering Rabaul Harbour. Scharnhorst leading, Leipzig, Nurnberg, Gneisenau, and Dresden on flank.

without giving them any preliminary warning at all, for this is the letter that Admiral Patey's messenger brought back:

> According to the principles of the rights of nations, especially of the agreements of the second Hague Peace Conference, the bombardment of our harbours and protectorates is forbidden, as is the threat to do so. I therefore respectfully protest against your Excellency's proposal. But to avoid the military measures you propose, I have given orders for the wireless telegraph station to be demolished and that no resistance shall be offered.

It always went against the grain with many Britishers that the last home of Stevenson, the island that has his grave on one of its hill-tops, should ever have been ceded to the Germans, and the news that it had been recovered from them was an occasion for enthusiastic rejoicing on that sentimental ground, as well as because it meant that a valuable colony had been added to the Empire.

One very pleasant circumstance in connection with this bloodless victory was that the French and British residents in the Samoan Islands bore testimony to the kindness with which they had been treated by the German authorities and spontaneously petitioned the conquerors to show special consideration to the German ex-governor and his officials, and the request was met at once in the friendliest possible spirit. It almost seemed as if the gracious, humane influence of Tusitala were still potent in the very atmosphere of the place. Colonel Robert Logan, the new British Administrator of Samoa, took up residence with his staff at Stevenson's own house "Vailima," which had been occupied by the German governor, Dr. Schultz, and says in his report:

> I conferred with the German heads of departments and their subordinates, and, as they have given their parole to do nothing inimical to British interests and to carry out their duties loyally, I have retained them, with two exceptions, in their respective offices at the same salaries as they were previously receiving.

Equally pleasant, too, in connection with the capture of Samoa, were certain details mentioned concerning the appointment of Mr. Williams to the post of Deputy-Administrator of the island of Savali. Colonel Logan wrote:

> Mr. Williams has been in the islands for over forty years, and from the inception of German rule in Samoa until the declaration of war acted in the capacity of Deputy Administrator of Savali, under the German Government. On the declaration of war, he was given the option of resigning his British citizenship or being relieved of his office, and he chose the latter alternative, although this entailed the loss of his pension.

The transfer of Samoa being arranged in this humane, reasonable fashion, the allied fleets departed to continue their other business, leaving a garrison of some 2,000 New Zealand troops at Apia in charge of the islands. A fortnight later those roving ships of the German Pacific squadron came round that way and shelled Apia, and were energetically shelled in return; but the firing did not last long; there was no attempt at a landing, very little damage was done, and ever since the New Zealanders have remained in peaceable possession of their first trophy.

In the interval, on the 11th September, at 7 in the morning, the Australian squadron occupied Herbertshohe, the principal town in the island of New Pomerania, which is the largest island of the Bismarck Archipelago. It was discovered by Captain Cook, who named it New Britain, but the British Government never formally took possession of it, and in 1884 Germany seized and rechristened it, and at the same time annexed half of the neighbouring island of New Guinea and changed its name to Kaiser Wilhelmsland.

The remainder of New Guinea had long been shared betwixt the Dutch and the British, and there was profound dissatisfaction in Australia when the Germans were thus allowed to steal a march on us. There was already a feeling abroad that they were hankering after world-dominion and were dangerous neighbours. This uneasiness had been lulled by the passing of years, but the aggressive boastfulness of Germany and the outbreak of the war had naturally revived it and sharpened it to more than its first acuteness, and the knowledge that this menace to her peace had been finally removed was received throughout Australia with a lively satisfaction that was echoed from every quarter of the Empire.

On that morning of the 11th September a party of fifty men of the Australian Naval Reserve, under the command of Commander J. A. H. Beresford, and accompanied by Lieutenant-Commander Elwell and Lieutenant Bowen, landed at Herbert-shohe. There was a small group of Germans gathered on the wharf, and these, being hailed, replied that no opposition would be offered.

As soon as the landing party had fallen in on the beach they set out to march through the forest to the wireless station, which was about six miles inland, and luckily, in spite of the Germans' assurance that they would meet with no resistance. Commander Beresford was on the alert against treachery, had thrown out scouts, and was prepared for any surprise attack that might be attempted. There was no sign or sound of an enemy for a while, but when they had gone some two miles into the forest the invaders suddenly realised that they had walked into a trap.

A volley fired from the bush and dense tropical undergrowth which shut the road in on either side took them unawares. A German force had entrenched themselves close ahead athwart the road, and a number of blacks, hidden among the trees on both sides, started and kept up a harassing enfilade. But the Australians took the half-expected surprise with the most perfect sangfroid. They energetically returned the enemy's fire with a raking volley or two, then hurled themselves on the trenches, and, after a furious hand-to-hand struggle, carried them at the point of the bayonet.

They captured several prisoners, and leaving these in a hut under a small guard the rest of the party pushed on resolutely, taking what cover was possible by the way and maintaining a continuous fight with snipers who kept pace with them, lurking in the depths of the forest. The advance was necessarily slow, for, in addition to the death that momentarily threatened them from among the trees, the road was mined in many places, and nothing but the utmost caution and coolness saved the indomitable little army from annihilation. As it was, they suffered heavy losses.

Within 500 yards of the wireless station they found themselves faced with more entrenchments and came to a halt. A careful reconnaissance was made, and the position discovered to be so powerfully fortified that a dispatch-runner was sent back to ask for reinforcements from the fleet, and as it was by now almost dark Commander Beresford decided to encamp for the night. All night scouts were out keeping a close watch, and the men slept beside their rifles, but nothing happened. Even the snipers remained silent; many had been shot down, and the rest had either used up their ammunition or withdrawn disheartened; and the entrenched Germans lay low, apparently contented to wait till they were attacked.

Before dawn a great cheer rang from the awakening camp as the expected reinforcements, a detachment of Australian sailors, were seen approaching along the forest road. They brought several quick-firers and some 12-pounders with them, but no sooner were the guns in position and a storming party in readiness to advance than the enemy blew up the station and fled. Shots were sent after them, but they escaped into the bush, and the pursuit was not continued, since the object of the Australian expedition had been to destroy the wireless equipment there, and this had been accomplished.

Later in the day, however, the enemy reappeared behind the town and indulged in some casual sniping, but a few well-placed shells from one of the warships in the harbour discouraged them and drove them back into the interior.

The fighting for the wireless station had occupied eighteen hours, and it fell into the hands of the Australians at 1 o'clock in the morning on the 12th September. Between twenty and thirty Germans were killed; there were many wounded, and the commandant and one other officer, fifteen German non-commissioned officers, and fifty-six native police were taken prisoners. The Australian losses were Lieutenant-Commander B. Elwell,

Captain B. A. Bockley, R.A.M.C., and four seamen killed, and Lieutenant Rowland B. Bowen and three seamen wounded.

The Governor of New Pomerania (now restored to its earlier name of New Britain) remained at large for a day or two, and then was captured with his suite ten miles inland, and they were sent as prisoners to the port of Rabaul.

The capture of this port of Rabaul was one of the most daring and successful episodes in the campaign on New Pomerania. It was thought possible that the German cruisers were somewhere in the vicinity, and the Australian commander had no knowledge of Rabaul Harbour, and knew nothing of its fortifications; nevertheless, with all lights out he raided the port at night, caught the Germans napping, and landed a naval force without opposition. They had taken possession of the post and telegraph stations and destroyed the plant before the inhabitants were roused and came out to find it was too late for them to attempt to do anything.

Some of the German residents subsequently refused to take the oath of neutrality, and these, with two German officers, were sent as prisoners to Sydney. There was also some little trouble with the natives, who resorted to a sort of guerilla warfare, but it was not long before these were reduced to order, and the Australian garrison remained in peaceable control of the island, which had been the centre of the German Government in the Bismarck Archipelago.

Whilst Rabaul was being raided, another Australian warship landed a small squad of sailors under the command of Lieutenant-Commander Bloomfield at Nauru, the capital of the Marshall Islands. With the party were Lieutenant Cooper, Engineer-Lieutenant Creswell, and Staff-Surgeon Brennard, to act as interpreter. The surf round the island is very heavy, and there were difficulties in getting a boat through it, but this once accomplished the rest was easy. There were no defences, and the landing was unopposed. The governor surrendered at discretion, and the wireless station, one of the most powerful in the German Pacific series, was demolished.

Shortly after the fall of Rabaul, the Australian fleet captured a German steamer that was making for the harbour there, and learned from two Englishmen who were aboard that the elusive German cruisers had recently been sighted off Kaweing, New Hanover. But though a warship was dispatched forthwith to that quarter and toured all about the islands, searching diligently, no enemy vessels were anywhere discoverable. They had been seen thereabouts a few days previously, but had mysteriously vanished again.

The conquest of the German Pacific islands was completed on 24th September, when Kaiser Wilhelmsland (German New Guinea) surrendered without firing a shot, the British flag was hoisted at Friedrich Wilhelm town, and a garrison established there. Most of the available German soldiers had been sent thence a fortnight before to assist in the defence of New Pomerania; but when they arrived it was already taken over by the victorious Australians and they simply fell into their hands as prisoners. The principal officials of Kaiser Wilhelmsland were also absent; the four that remained, with some fourteen other Germans, took the oath of neutrality.

So, with every German wireless station in the Pacific put out of action, and the British flag flying over all enemy territory in those waters, the Australian fleet was free to render more assistance to the New Zealand, the British, and French fleets in their dogged hunt after the German commerce raiders, and presently added a new glory to its name by overtaking, giving battle to, and sinking that most dashing raider of them all, the *Emden*.

THE TRIUMPH OF THE SYDNEY

When we are all at peace again—when the Great War is a thing of yesterday and tales of its thousand fights have passed into the history and folklore of the nations that took part in it—then, I think, perhaps Germany may be glad to forget about the hundreds of women and children slaughtered by her runaway warships in bombarding defenceless English coast towns without warning, by her midnight Zeppelins with bombs that were dropped on peaceful villages and unfortified towns, by the torpedoes fired by her dishonoured submarines into helpless passenger steamers; but she will find consolation and some healing for her pride in remembering the brilliant exploits of the *Emden*, and the splendid chivalry and heroism of the *Emden's* commander.

She will talk of Karl von Müller, and rightly, much as we talk of Drake and Hawkins, or as the Americans talk of that daring privateer Paul Jones, and of Captain Semmes and the *Alabama*. But his enemies were the first to pay tribute to his gallantry and welcome him into the glorious company of their traditional sea-heroes; for such courage as his naturalises an alien even in the land of his enemy, and, for all the harm he did us, we have nothing but the friendliest admiration of von Müller, because he harried and fought us with clean hands and was always a gracious and honourable as well as a fearless foe.

At the outbreak of the war, the German admiral, von Spec, was at Kiao-Chau with his China squadron of some half-dozen vessels. He lost no time in putting to sea, bent on preying upon and, as far as might be, stopping the ocean-trade of Britain and France and their Allies. Before long he seems to have decided to set von Müller free to follow his own devices; the *Emden* parted company with the admiral and thereafter, playing a lone hand, proved a more resourceful and more dangerous marauder than all the rest of von Spec's fleet put together. For three months it cruised about the Pacific and the Indian Oceans and was the terror of the seas.

Today it would be sighted off Borneo, and whilst the Australian and New Zealand fleets, called by wireless, were scouring the China Sea for it, it would unexpectedly appear off the Caroline Islands or in the Bay of Bengal. It left its mark on the harbour works of Madras, shelled the fort there and set the oil-tanks ablaze, and was gone into the unknown again before any pursuer could be put on its track. And all the while its gallant captain was making sudden dashes into those ocean highways where the merchant traffic was thickest, taking toll of our traders with the gayest good humour and always with the strictest consideration for the lives of his victims.

Our experts assured us that this game could not last; sooner or later von Müller would have to put into port somewhere for coal and stores, news of his whereabouts would be flashed to the ships in chase of him and they would be waiting in readiness for him when he came out, and there would be an end of him. It sounded so simple and true, but von Müller knew a trick worth two of that. His practice was to bear down upon his quarry, make her heave to by sending a shot across her bows, then board her and help himself to what he needed in the way of coal and other stores, transfer the crew and passengers to the *Emden*, and sink his abandoned prize with a bomb or with a well-aimed shell or two.

After he had repeated this proceeding so many times that he had more prisoners aboard than he could comfortably accommodate, he dumped them all on the next merchantman he overhauled and allowed it to go free with them. He was so good a sailor, and knew the sea and the ways of the sea so well, that, instead of making his captures one by one, he occasionally contrived to round up four or five at a time, shepherded them into suitable proximity, went through them in succession, helped himself liberally from their cargoes, collected all the passengers and crews on one of them, which he politely set at liberty, and swiftly sunk the remainder and was off again about his business.

He had a sense of humour, and that invariably goes with humanity. One of the ships he stopped was a small affair with no particularly valuable cargo, so he relinquished it intact, jestingly making a present of it to the wife of the captain, who was making the voyage with her husband. History does not say whether the owners subsequently confirmed the gift. He discovered that there were women among the passengers on another ship, and, genially apologising for causing them any discomfort, withdrew and let his catch go again.

Many such stories were rumoured about him, and even if some were legendary the fact that it occurred to his enemies to tell them sufficiently indicates the character of the man. His luck and his daring and his courtesy made a sort of popular hero of him even in the British Isles and Australasia, but the damage he was doing to our shipping was so serious that it became more and more imperative that his career should be ended. By an ingenious ruse he sunk a French destroyer and a Russian cruiser at Penang; and, to say nothing else of our Allies' losses, he had destroyed over 74,000 tons of British shipping, the total value of which has been estimated at upwards of £2,000,000, before he was brought to bay, and put up a good fight, but was beaten.

His little cruiser could make a speed of twenty-four knots, and so long as he kept out at sea, he was able to show his pursuers a clean pair of heels. Possibly his three months of immunity had rendered him a little over-confident; anyhow, it occurred to him that he might increase the difficulties of the chase by destroying the wireless plant on Keeling Cocos Island, and at 6 o'clock on the morning of the 9th November he carried out his intention. He sent an armed launch ashore, towing two boats containing forty men, three officers, and four maxims. They effected a landing without trouble in a quarter of an hour; the officers behaved with the correctest courtesy towards the officials and damaged nothing but the wireless installation, which they very efficiently reduced to ruins.

But it happened that an hour earlier the approach of the *Emden* had been detected, and the wireless operator had immediately flung a warning into the air and an urgent appeal to the *Sydney*, which was believed to be somewhere in the vicinity. This belief was so well founded that as the expeditionary force from the *Emden* were returning to their boats, after completing their mission, a dense smoke was seen on the horizon, and breaking through it the *Sydney*, coming under full steam, hove rapidly into sight.

Captain von Müller was as quick to observe it, recognised that there was no escape, and instantly prepared for action. Leaving his landing party to look after themselves, he steamed for the open sea, and his men on shore with equal promptitude commandeered a schooner that lay at anchor in the bay, hastily provisioned it, cut the cable, made a dash for liberty and got away.

As soon as she was clear of the island the *Emden* opened fire on the *Sydney* and at first made excellent practice, but the *Sydney* answered by pouring in such an accurate and deadly fire that the enemy's three funnels were shot away, some of his guns silenced, and all the speaking-tubes smashed, so that the captain had difficulties in transmitting his orders, and his firing began to fall off considerably. If there were pluck and determination enough on the *Emden*, there was at least as much of both on her antagonist. For three months the *Sydney* had been kept waiting for this hour, with her crew spoiling for a fight, and now they had got what they had been waiting for, and officers and men alike were keen to render a good account of themselves. Before the *Sydney* left the harbour, she was named after, three boys came aboard from the training ship *Tingua* and offered themselves as volunteers for service in any capacity.

The captain thought they were too young and did not want to take them, but they were so desperately bent on going that he yielded and let them have their way. Two of them were now attached to the officers of the gun crew, and throughout the action with the *Emden* they were as eager and as perfectly cool as the hardiest seaman of them all. One of these youngsters was told off to help in carrying ammunition to the guns, and he went briskly, capably to and fro on his job, with the enemy's shells bursting around and overhead, and never even seemed to think of attempting to take cover. The fearful joy of battle possessed him as it possessed the rest of the crew. The cheerfulness and reckless ardour of them all were amazing; nobody thought of danger; nobody thought of anything except that they were at grips with the enemy at long last and did not mean to let him go.

It was a short, sharp, heroic combat; there was no flinching on either side; but the *Sydney's* guns were the more powerful and her gunners the better marksmen. She was very little damaged and her only loss was three men killed and fifteen wounded; but the *Emden* was so terribly punished that her decks became a very shambles; there were over two hundred killed and wounded, and the finish came when the whole after-part of the vessel burst into flames. The *Sydney* at once ceased firing, and von Müller threw up the sponge and smartly beached his ship to save it from sinking.

The Britishers ashore and rescue parties in the *Sydney's* boats assisted to get the wounded out of the blazing wreck, and, accepting the inevitable with his customary good grace, the German captain surrendered. But Captain Glossop, the *Sydney's* commander, knew how to respect a brave enemy and refused to deprive his beaten foe of his sword. It was characteristic of von Müller that when one of his officers, smarting under the sense of defeat, accused the *Sydney* of continuing to fire after the white flag had been shown, he called the remnant of his forces together and repeated the charge to them, only to repudiate it indignantly, saying that no white flag had ever been hoisted on his vessel.

He and the *Kaiser's* kinsman. Prince Franz Joseph Hohenzollern, with the rest of the captured German officers and men, were sent as prisoners of war to Australia, and the most romantic and one of the most momentous episodes in the war at sea came to a fitting conclusion when the vast crowd which gathered at Sydney Harbour to welcome with storms of cheering the triumphant Captain Glossop and his men, broke into a generous ovation for the hero of the *Emden* as his conquerors brought him in.

The Indian and Pacific Oceans were now swept completely clear of all enemies, except for the small German fleet that was still groping about precariously off Chili, and on the 8th December a British squadron drew this fleet into an engagement and totally destroyed it; but the significance of the *Sydney's* dashing victory was not merely that it removed the last serious menace from the ocean trade routes of the Empire—it created the profoundest impression throughout India, and did more to restore confidence among our Indian fellow-subjects in the eventual triumph of British arms than the hurling back of the German hordes from before the walls of Paris or the greater successes of our navy in the North Sea.

www.ingramcontent.com/pod-product-compliance
Lightning Source LLC
Chambersburg PA
CBHW031854090426
42741CB00005B/491